THE VALUE vs FORCE™ EDUCAT

RECEIVABILITY

9 Steps to Apply Quantum Physics for Your Success

DARYLLE VIRGINIA DENNIS

Be a
RISING TIDE
Publishing

Denver, Colorado

Receivability: 9 Steps to Apply Quantum Physics for Your Success
Published by Be A Rising Tide Publishing
Denver, CO

Copyright © 2020 by Darylle Virginia Dennis. All rights reserved.

No part of this book may be reproduced in any form or by any mechanical means, including information storage and retrieval systems without permission in writing from the publisher/author, except by a reviewer who may quote passages in a review.

All images, logos, quotes, and trademarks included in this book are subject to use according to trademark and copyright laws of the United States of America.

ISBN: 978-1-7347893-0-0

BUSINESS / Knowledge Capital

Cover and Interior design by Wolf Design and Marketing
All rights reserved by Darylle Virginia Dennis and Be A Rising Tide Publishing.

QUANTITY PURCHASES: Schools, companies, professional groups, clubs, and other organizations may qualify for special terms when ordering quantities of this title. For information, email Darylle@VALUEvsFORCE.com.

Printed in the United States of America.

CONTENTS

Introduction 1

Clarity 9

Why Do We Want this Goal? 19

Judgment 29

Impact Awareness 41

Access Intuitive Intelligence 49

Gratitude 73

Visualize 91

Detachment 101

Contribution 117

"I can teach anybody how to get what they want out of life. The problem is that I can't find anybody who can tell me what they want."

—MARK TWAIN

INTRODUCTION

DR. PETER DRUCKER

"Intelligence, imagination and knowledge are essential resources, but only effectiveness converts them into results. By themselves, they only set limits to what can be attained."

"A rising tide lifts all boats" is a centuries-old Chinese quote made famous by President John F. Kennedy in 1963. Several presidents have used this quote in broader macroeconomic terms, suggesting that when there is an improved economy, those participating in society will benefit from the rise of the overall economic improvement.

Microeconomics is the study of the effects on the economy from single factors, and the effects of individual decisions and actions. When an individual decides to improve their life by establishing goals to achieve, and they reach those goals, that individual becomes the influencer of *"a rising tide…"*

When we improve our own conditions, we do not tend to think of ourselves as individuals who are responsible for improved conditions for others; however, we are responsible whether we are aware of it or not.

An example of this truth is the famous runner Roger Bannister, who was the first to break the four-minute mile on May 6, 1954. Doctors, trainers, coaches, family and friends kept bombarding Bannister with all the reasons not to pursue his goal. They said the human body was not physiologically capable of being pushed to those extremes, and if he continued, he surely would die.

Once Bannister broke the four-minute mile for the world to see, he *raised the tide* for others as to what is possible, even though this was not his intention. Roger Bannister's breakthrough opened a channel for others to find passage beyond their current belief limitations, although

Introduction

Bannister's only intention was to build the channel for his own passage. (*A channel, by definition, is an opening that permits passage, whether for water or a band of frequencies.*)

Bannister was building the channel each day that he determined to reach his goal, and each moment he trained. Others who followed him had access to the now-proven passage to achieve their own goals.

Six weeks later, John Landy broke Bannister's record. Since then, more than 1,400 people have surpassed Bannister's record.

Roger Bannister became instrumental in contributing to *"a rising tide . . ."* in the running world, and is a fine example of determination and commitment for all those around him and those who have come after him, regardless of the field of work or play.

Consider making a leap of belief that each one of us who has accomplished a breakthrough raises the potential for others. Breakthroughs are advances in the development of our own emotional and psychological makeup. Raising the potential for others is an effect of our own breakthroughs.

> *"Triumph over fear is at the root of all breakthroughs."*
> —Darylle Virginia Dennis

The individual who conquers fear also experiences victory and liberation in broader areas of life. The individual's victory touches and "speaks" to the collective consciousness of the many, which is how breakthroughs influence. The individual's breakthrough built the channel, which makes it easier for those who come after.

All those to whom we are connected and all those who come after us will surely benefit from "*a rising tide*" that we caused with our own achievements, whether we are aware of this or not. We are instrumental in effecting *"a rising tide"* for others to achieve breakthroughs in the same areas of our own. Those others then become *"a rising tide"* for still others desiring breakthroughs, as well, and so on and so on it goes!

As we journey through our lives, many opportunities exist where we feel stuck and we want breakthroughs. Bursting out of a stuck place could be made easier when we understand two truths.

One: If you are having struggles of any kind, know that many others have the same struggles throughout the world. It may be challenging to wrap our heads around this idea that our "wins" *raise the tide* for others to benefit; however, this is true, and it is happening whether we are aware of it or not.

Two: The accomplishment of our breakthroughs will contribute to *"a rising tide,"* liberating others from their own stuckness, with or without our knowledge.

Realizing that our breakthrough is contributing to others, *"a rising tide lifts all boats,"* and becoming conscious of our impact, will generate additional power, no matter what the obstacle. This can accelerate our ability to break through due to the intention to liberate others from their sufferings.

The Nine-Step Effective Goal Receiving Practice, offered monthly, will open channels for dreams and objectives to break through any stuckness of any form. Our breakthroughs will become realized with surprisingly minimal effort.

For those who are convinced that setting goals does not work, this powerful, transformational goal exercise will surely change minds; the results received will leave no doubt.

When we created this goal exercise, the first assignment was to correct the name of this practice. After all, "goal setting" isn't even the goal of any goal exercise. The goal is to "goal receive," not to merely goal set.

The fundamentals of launching intentions and receiving goals require our participation. What we are about to learn is quite different than the traditional means to accomplishing goals. The following Nine-Step Practices we are about to share are not strategies from the volume of "doings," but rather from the clarity of "intendings!"

The long-standing teachings of how to accomplish goals have their share of effectiveness challenges on several levels. One of the challenges is thinking and deciding what we want and then believing that all we need to do is write it down. Writing down goals is similar to a to-do list, which is not nearly enough to bring something from the invisible into the visible. It is an excellent start, and better than wishing and hoping; however, our participation is required to bring the dream into the actual.

Another long-standing teaching, once decisions have been made on a goal, is to post pictures of the goal in multiple locations as a reminder of what you want. This goal step is ineffective. *(It's an interesting idea to post pictures as a reminder of what we want, but if we truly desire the goal, why do we require a regular reminder?)*

The picture of the goal on the bathroom mirror, on the laptop home screen, on the door leading into the garage and on the car dashboard actually creates overstimulation, which ends up desensitizing or numbing the strong desire to receive the goal. This step is ineffective and unnecessary.

A classic example could be having a treadmill in your home that you received as a gift. The New Year brings new goals to get into shape. Possibly by mid-February, the treadmill is used to drape clothing that you are going to take to the cleaners when you have extra time. Seeing the treadmill covered in clothes day in and day out, relatively soon, you no longer see the clothes OR the treadmill.

Posting pictures of the goal is not necessary to affect receiving the goal. The goal receiving practices offered here will teach and prove how unnecessary and ineffective it is to post goal pictures in a bombardment strategy.

What is missing in the goal examples, starting with the concept of goal setting as compared to goal receiving, is a lack of understanding of the power of intention.

Writing a goal with an intention of *"something to get"* is like a to-do list, which holds minimal thought and effort. One of the dictionary definitions of intention is: *"a generator of power; to produce."* It is also defined as: *"a thought; quality of purposefulness."* The Power of Intention is the generator of power that brings something from the invisible into the visible.

An aspect of bringing the unseen into the seen begins with intending with visual clarity. Visualize the goal as if your goal is already seen, already visible, already actual.

Intentions are powerful because they make things move. Begin every desired breakthrough with a visual moving picture of what your "seen" intention looks like. This is the birthing dynamic of bringing the non-material into the material, bringing the unseen into the seen.

This Value vs. Force Educational Series™ teaches effectiveness and productivity in a myriad of scenarios, together with the principles guiding the practices for desired outcomes. The internal and external attitudes and practices we teach in this series are the necessary characteristics of converting goals into results.

> *"Capitalism works even better if people are conscious. Just as an engineer who knows what she is doing can use a computer more effectively than someone who doesn't understand the technology, a conscious capitalist can participate in a free market more effectively than someone who doesn't understand its economic principles."*
> —Fred Kofman, PhD

INTRODUCTION

"Life by Design or Life by Default—Choose"

_____
_____
_____
_____
_____
_____
_____
_____
_____
_____
_____
_____
_____
_____
_____
_____
_____

*"Receive – 'to receive' is to allow, to let in or to greet;
to consent, to give opportunity."*

**PERSONAL – FINANCIAL – PROFESSIONAL
PHYSICAL – SPIRITUAL**

"Intelligence, imagination and knowledge are essential resources, but only effectiveness converts them into results. By themselves, they only set limits to what can be attained."

—Dr. Peter Drucker

step one

Clarity

"LIFE BY DESIGN"

Webster's Dictionary defines receive:
'to receive' is to allow, to let in or to greet; 'to allow' is to permit;
'to permit' is to consent, to give opportunity, to allow to be done.

"I can teach anybody how to get what they want out of life. The problem is that I can't find anybody who can tell me what they want."
—Mark Twain

Mark Twain was born in 1835, and what is remarkable to find in this quote is the clarity he illuminates regarding his current-day culture in the 1800s, and how true it still is today.

Clarity is the most significant component of bringing the non-visible into the visible. Clarity establishes whether an individual is living a "life by design" or a "life by default." A "life by design" is proactive, and a "life by default" is reactive.

Proactive is self-determination; reactive is compliance and obedience. Proactive generates energy; reactive spends energy.

Dreaming up a goal to accomplish, a never-before-imagined one, erupts creative energy and excitement never felt before.

On most occasions, the life force energy of creativity flowing through us is accompanied by Intuitive Intelligence, which enhances the vision and the possibilities. This is the good stuff of being alive!

The objective of clarity is to take some time and dig in deeper to explore the desired goals and objectives that we truly want to fulfill. This fulfillment occurs in five fundamental areas of our lives:

Personal – Financial – Professional – Physical – Spiritual.

The first exercise is to define in each fundamental area what you would like/love to experience, have and enjoy. Be specific and literal, as this is essential to your outcomes. Being specific speaks to the dynamic of creating a *"life by design."*

A "life by default" is *"hoping to have a good day," "hoping to receive enough money to get through the month," "hoping everything works out," or "hoping to get the business needed for a quota."* Subconsciously, a *"life by default"* becomes bracing oneself to handle whatever comes along, to be prepared for the unknown. This dynamic is where drama scenarios live. The unexpected can feel similar to being victimized. The unexpected can, many times, be the unwanted. The unwanted can so easily turn into the unfair.

"Life by default" is more challenging to live each day, and it can seem like hard work to be happy, healthy and abundant.

You can make a simple shift in Step One. Take time to get clear on what you desire, and the other eight steps, if applied, will ensure a complete *"life by design."* The result will be abundance in all areas of your life in a dream-come-true manner! This is not an idle promise. Quantum physicists have proven, in case studies around the world, that our lives have the power to create, expand and resolve anything and everything on which we place our attention. Together with our belief in what is possible, the desired results will most surely occur.

CLARITY MATTERS

PRACTICAL APPLICATION

A twist of fate changed the direction of my career in October 2005.

The beginning of my career was in commercial banking as a business development officer with Imperial Bank. The marketing department, with 125 business development people, would go into business communities and invite corporations to bank with Imperial Bank. This was a tremendous opportunity for me to learn about every possible type of business.

My experiences with so many different companies provided unlimited growth in every possible way. It was an astounding opportunity, especially as I was a very young woman in higher levels of executive banking.

From the beginning, I was fascinated by the dynamics present when being productive and effective. The intensity of my commitment to excel in business and life opened doors that led to consulting for community banks, as well as corporate clients I had developed over several years. My consulting contracts usually were for companies to improve productivity, effectiveness and results.

The twist of fate I could never have seen coming was an invitation to speak at a small luncheon for NAPMW, the National Association of Professional Mortgage Women in Phoenix, Arizona. The president had said the scheduled speaker was not available to attend the next day, and asked if I would fill in. This was September 9, 2005.

As much as I tried to convince the president that I did not do public speaking, she said, *"You seem to be good at marketing, so talk about that."* There were twenty-one attendees in this small luncheon. The luncheon speech was thirty minutes. Right after the talk, a young woman came up and said how much she enjoyed the presentation, and had never heard anyone talk about those concepts in a business setting. She asked if we could meet.

The twist of fate came the moment this brilliant young woman walked up and asked to meet. She was the national sales director of a company in Michigan. Her sales team covered the country. Her strategy was to attract larger audiences and take what she heard at the luncheon and develop it into a three-hour presentation. Then, she would potentially accomplish two goals at one time.

Her sales team would be in front of several hundred potential clients, and this teaching could be of high value to those attending. The value it could bring to those attending would then open doors for her company. This brilliant director of marketing encouraged her team to book me in every major city across the U.S. For the next three years, the teaching and practices offered in the Value vs. Force **Educational** Series™ opened hearts and minds across America to the concepts of Value Exchange Dynamics™.

Now, being in a new business, I needed a new model and a website to communicate this teaching and how it would benefit those attending seminars, workshops and classes. My goal was to find a website developer. Web development was still very new in 2005. Ultimately, I paid five different developers $2,500 each for a website and logo. I received a logo from the third developer and nothing from the other four. I was very frustrated and became more than annoyed that this was taking so long, and for whatever reason, could not seem to find the right support team for my new business.

From my frustration and disappointment, I got very clear on what I wanted, and stated these specific requests out loud:

- Find a quality web developer.
- Pay them as soon as they create a website to my satisfaction.
- Not pay one more dime to anyone until I receive what I asked for as a speaker and consultant.
- Once I have received what I asked for, then and only then will I pay the invoice for their services.
- AND I want to find this ideal web developer before the sun sets TODAY!

My clarity and determination for this goal to be fulfilled came early in the morning before I left for a consulting project. When I arrived at the company where I was working, I ran into one of the salespeople. I briefly asked if she knew of anyone who would develop a website and be paid after they completed their design of the site. She said no, and I added that I had paid five different web developers and now cannot locate them and was saddened by the seeming lack of accountability in this new industry.

The Result of Clarity

A couple of hours went by, and the salesperson I ran into earlier experienced her car breaking down, which was unusual as it was a new Cadillac Escalade. She ultimately ended up at Enterprise Car Rental and was in line to rent a car. The man in front of her had flown in from France, and was complaining about how slow the service was for people usually in a hurry.

This French man, named George, asked her what she did for a living. She shared and then asked him about his profession. He said, *"I am a web developer!"* She was shocked and shared my brief story of hiring five developers and receiving only a logo from one of them. George said, *"Actually I am a web developer for Ball Aerospace and eBay, and do not work with small independent businesses. However, what has happened to this woman is unacceptable and gives my industry a bad name. If you would please give me her contact information, I will call her."*

At 3:15 p.m., a call comes into my cell phone, and it is George. George relayed the story of meeting this woman at Enterprise Car Rental and what she had told him about my frustrations.

George then said, *"Even though I work with very large corporations, I have resources throughout the country of web developers who I trust and refer business to when smaller projects are requested."*

He went on to say, *"I know of a wonderful web developer in Oregon named Gisele, and she is incredible. I will ask her to call you and give you whatever you ask for. I will instruct her to not ask for any money until you are thoroughly and entirely satisfied. Once you say what she developed is what you want, then and only then can she invoice you. I will also add, if for any reason you do not pay, I will pay her."*

I was speechless beyond belief. What this total stranger said matched the clarity of requests in the five itemized areas of my goals that I had set earlier that morning. All of this happened before sunset that same day!

By the way, the website Gisele developed was stunning! She worked night and day until it was completed… in record time too!

This experience could appear as some remarkable coincidence; however, I have learned beyond any doubt that the clearer we are when establishing what we want, the faster it becomes real. This process of clarifying goals, then experiencing the speed at which they arrive, means we are now left with an incredible knowing that we have the capability and the power to create a full business and a full *"life by design."*

STEP ONE: CLARITY

"Triumph over fear is at the root of all breakthroughs."
—DARYLLE VIRGINIA DENNIS

_____
_____
_____
_____
_____
_____
_____
_____
_____
_____
_____
_____
_____
_____
_____
_____
_____
_____
_____

"Intention is a generator of power; to produce."
—DICTIONARY DEFINITION

**PERSONAL – FINANCIAL – PROFESSIONAL
PHYSICAL – SPIRITUAL**

"Once you discover your WHY, you are better able to align your beliefs with every choice and action you take, in order to find greater fulfillment in all that you do."

—Simon Sinek

step two

WHY DO WE WANT THIS GOAL?

SIMON SINEK

"Once you discover your WHY, you are better able to align your beliefs with every choice and action you take, in order to find greater fulfillment in all that you do."

Step Two is about working to discover why we want the goal, and this is significant to the quality and speed of the outcome. Why, in essence, is defined as a reason, cause or purpose. The reason why we want the goal must be guided by the truth of our why to be able to bring the invisible into the visible. The "why" we want a specific goal goes directly to the root of the desire: no interference. It's similar to a clear channel, a clear signal, which is why knowing our why is so powerful.

Our why, when based in passion, will produce an outcome in the speed of light. Heartmath Institute has revealed in thousands of case studies, that how we feel is five thousand times more powerful an energy than any other energy that could be expressed by a human being.

If we were to offer an alternative truth of why we want the goal, and replace it with an ideological goal, the energy would be restrained and the outcome stalled in the process: all due to a lack of truthful clarity.

An ideological goal could be for $5 million, and our why could be to contribute to a worthy cause and provide resources to help the needy; however, the true reason may be to handle many financial matters that are burdening and escalating in stress, loss and fear. Our internal integrity knows our issues, our concerns and our true desires for the goal.

Many have the misunderstanding that *"the more pure and lofty our reasons are for the goal, the faster it will come."* The dynamics of unambiguous power will impact an outcome with speed through the truth of our why. *"The truth will set you free"* is deeper, richer and more than we have come to truly understand. The truth is freedom from all that confines.

Not having our fundamental needs met interferes with achieving our loftier, higher goals, which are bigger than ourselves. Let's get the abundance for ourselves handled and get on with the business of why we are here. This is the intention of the goal receiving exercises within The Power of Goal Receiving.

The Gap Period

"Our creative genius and artistry are expressed inside and during the Gap Period." —Darylle Virginia Dennis

The Gap is the period of time in between the goal being defined and the goal appearing in the material world. We frequently misinterpret the in-between time as *"nothing is happening, and there is no evidence to be seen for this goal arriving anytime soon."* The mind automatically defaults to negativity when it does not have information. The in-between time is when our participation matters the most in the Goal Receiving exercises.

Our doubts from a lack of information begin to create a self-fulfilling prophecy. Self-talk, such as, *"This isn't happening. Goal setting doesn't work. It never has. Why would now be any different? Maybe I set the bar too high,"* becomes the negativity the mind makes up without any visible evidence of something happening.

The other part of the mind that goes on autopilot is the belief that it must be right about everything all the time. The mind is concocting evaluations, which we make without a scintilla of evidence.

If you are not receiving what you want, you have more doubt and lack in your attitude than you have in your expectations. Expectations are the power source that brings the invisible into the visible. Lack of information creates doubt.

The Gap Period is energetically responding to the goal we defined, which is moving and evolving by the force of our why, and is in the middle of becoming real.

The Gap is a sacred space where what we do, think and feel gives birth to a new reality, which also becomes a new reality for those who come after us: *"a rising tide lifts all boats."* This is a practice of bringing the invisible into the visible.

A key to a goal becoming real and for the goal to arrive bigger, better and more than we requested, has everything to do with what we do and how we think and feel during the Gap Period.

Think of ordering a wonderful dinner with someone in a special restaurant. Once you have made your request, you are enjoying the time in between ordering and until the dinner arrives.

This is the key to setting and receiving goals, no matter how long it takes.

The requesting or "ordering" of the goal is not that different than ordering a dinner. The in-between time period of the Gap is not that different, either. In and during the Gap Period and until the goal arrives, enjoy the in-between time with your loved ones, your clients or others with whom you might be dining.

Think and feel in terms of high expectations and excitement that the goal is on its way, and what joy you will feel when it does arrive. That's all there is to it!

Starting from a thought and a dream, unseen is becoming seen and experienced. Know for sure: we did that! Our creative genius and artistry are expressed inside and during the Gap Period. The in-between period of the Gap is the best of experiences!

The energy we are emitting is watering the Vibrational Garden in the Gap. During the Gap Period, we simply must look through a mode of receiving…a mode of expectation.

Practical Application

Commercial business development banking has been the love of my life for a long time. Everything I have learned from the men and women who taught me invaluable lessons has contributed to the quality of my life. The vastness of my exposure to the corporate world is incredibly rare for most professions.

During every vacation I took as a young person to new cities, states and countries, I would always stop and walk into a bank and ask to meet the management, as I would love to hear how they do their business development and marketing. Walking into The Bank of Montreal in Vancouver, Canada, as a twenty-two-year-old, was a high point. They were excited to hear about our marketing efforts. *"How bold,"* they said, when I shared our proactive marketing activities and the incredible value of the experiences! They did not, at that time, have marketing in banking available in Canada. I felt as fortunate as I ever could have imagined feeling. Each evening I asked, *"How did I get this lucky?"*

Fast-forward to now, after I've been an international speaker and consultant, and I am still very interested in speaking with and for banking communities and independent banks. Astounding new methodologies are pouring out of MIT, Harvard, Stanford and Wharton School of Business regarding business growth and development, as well as new management strategies, and I am craving to share them all with bankers!

During a Goal Receiving exercise, I launched an intention to speak at a bankers association luncheon. Following the visualization practices in goal receiving, I knew that visualization was a significant aspect of the quality and speed at which goals arrive. I could clearly see the room in my mind. One hundred and twenty-five bank presidents were there. My visual showed me standing behind a podium—which I rarely do because I like to have nothing in between me and the audience—however, it's what came up in the *"movie"* I was creating in my mind. Seeing the faces of the presidents riveted to the subjects I presented was breathtaking, and imagining how this new approach would impact the growth of their banks was a fantastic feeling!

I shared my "why" with these presidents in my visual movie, and clearly stated my "why" in my mind: *"From bankers like yourselves, who taught me everything that changed the quality of my life, now I have an opportunity to give back and say thank you from the bottom of my heart for all I have learned and gained because of you. This is why I am passionate about banking and passionate about you and passionate about why I am here! Thank you!"*

At this time, I was consulting with a mortgage banking firm in San Ramon, California. Their presence was in eight states, and one of their unique services was to perform a private label mortgage lending service for small independent banks. One of my roles was to open opportunities for small banks to benefit by offering permanent lending to their customers. Until this program was made available, smaller community banks would refer their clients who needed permanent lending to larger competitor banks for mortgage lending services. Often, the larger banks would recruit the smaller bank's clients to their bank, which had far more resources for customer service. This new program would reduce the number of clients that smaller banks lost to larger banks.

This was a fantastic program that I was passionate about for the smaller independent banks.

I scheduled a Monday morning appointment with a small community bank's CEO, and I was looking forward to offering this program to a bank that had lost several clients to larger competitor banks because the clients were seeking permanent financing.

The CEO and I met in their conference room, and he seemed enthusiastic about my client's program providing lending services for their customers without them having to do anything regarding mortgage lending, which was of no interest, nor was mortgage lending this bank's skill set.

As I was getting up to leave, the CEO said, *"You seem to be passionate about banking. Why?"* Instantly, I repeated what was in my visual "movie" in my head during the earlier Goal Receiving exercise, but in a shorter version:

"From bankers like yourself, who taught me everything that changed the quality of my life, now I have an opportunity to give back and say thank you from the bottom of my heart for all I have learned and gained because of you. This is why I am passionate about banking!"

What completely took me by storm was his next response. He said, *"I am on the Board of Directors of the Independent Bankers Association, and we are always looking for luncheon speakers. May I refer you to the woman who puts our programs together?"*

I left the CEO's bank high as a kite. How powerful and simple was the process that these exercises offer, to define a clear goal and add the concept of "why" as a power source. This was amazing! A wonderful firsthand experience! It's true: "whys" matter! The truth of our desires lives in our "whys." It's an unstoppable combination for making dreams come true!

STEP TWO: WHY DO WE WANT THIS GOAL

"a rising tide lifts all boats." —UNKNOWN

_____
_____
_____
_____
_____
_____
_____
_____
_____
_____
_____
_____
_____
_____
_____
_____
_____

"Why is the catalyst that leads to passion and fulfillment."
—DARYLLE VIRGINIA DENNIS

PERSONAL – FINANCIAL – PROFESSIONAL
PHYSICAL – SPIRITUAL

"The primary cause of suffering is not the events that have happened in our lives. The primary cause of suffering is our judgments about the events that have happened in our lives."

—Darylle Virginia Dennis

step three

JUDGMENT

DARYLLE VIRGINIA DENNIS

"The primary cause of suffering is not the events that have happened in our lives. The primary cause of suffering is our judgments about the events that have happened in our lives."

This workshop intends to empower and enable people to live fulfilled, abundant lives. Defined characteristics are at work, and they determine whether we are empowered or victimized. Both possibilities are from choice, and we make preferred choices when we have a deeper understanding of how we work and the underlying causes of each choice.

So many people have pursued liberation from limitations for so many years. Limitations originate from beliefs and judgments that prohibit any possibility of breaking free from constraints. This workshop provides the internal attitudes and external methodologies for the freedom to express your fullest potential. You will be able to utilize your own magnificence to build your business and your life, and in the process, make an indelible difference for all those who cross your path.

Dr. Abraham Maslow, a behavioral scientist, discovered that the human being's core identity and drive to be alive is to manifest our full potential. This is the deepest craving of every human being.

Those who have revealed and released their potential are making profound and significant impacts on generations and cultures worldwide. Even those who are unaware of their potential are making a difference when interacting with others. The quality of the impact they make depends on the state of mind and life condition of each individual.

Dramatic shifts are currently taking place in all aspects of our society in the United States and around the globe. These shifts are in developmental stages now and are vying for relevance, and in some cases, dominance. If the developmental processes of these shifts come from our higher potentials, and not our egos, then the outcomes of these shifts will be more enduring.

Our collective contributions originating from our full potentials are capable of building a world of magnificence, beauty, abundance and unity. For this to be possible, we need to shift from ego-based decision-making to value-based decision-making. Value-based decision-making begins with value-driven intentions and assessments, as compared to good-bad, right-wrong-based intentions and assessments.

One characteristic of bringing forth our full potential begins with an intention to be of value to others—others being our clients, colleagues, friends and families. Intention is a *"generator of power; to produce."*

When intention is applied to be of value to another, that specific intent stimulates the qualities within our own potentials. The untapped, unused qualities of our potentials emerge in the present moment and serve a unique value, which is specific for the one you are meeting. Once we stimulate our untapped potential, and it surfaces, it becomes an ever-present quality of our character, never to go dormant again.

In a business setting, the outcomes from these developmental practices evoking our potentials are nothing short of miraculous.

Business development within our careers provides bountiful opportunities to engage, polish and improve our potentials. People fundamentally want to be heard, understood and appreciated. When we communicate these intentions of value toward another, our business accelerates in quantum leaps.

What is happening when the outcome of our efforts to build and grow our businesses evades us?

Judgment of some form is happening, perhaps toward situations or others. Whatever the judgment is and regardless of the reason, the negativity that judgment causes will be powerfully felt and interpreted by others. Business flows through people. When exuding judgment for any reason, those around us may interpret it as judgment toward them, and it's an unwelcoming feeling.

Judgment is more powerful than we realized in the past. Many are completely unaware of how much judgment affects the outcomes of their efforts. People say all the time, *"I am working hard and not stopping until I improve my results."* Working hard is not the solution to the circumstance of not having enough business. We will find the solution when we take a deeper look at our attitudes, beliefs and judgments.

Building our businesses and improving our relationships will be an outgrowth of people feeling good around us. Here's a related quote that has been attributed to Maya Angelou: *"People will forget what you said, people will forget what you did, but people will never forget how you made them feel."* We cannot hide our judgments, but we can transform them into energies and attitudes of appreciation, no matter what caused the judgment in the first place.

Eckhart Tolle, in his book, *A New Earth, Awakening to Your Life's Purpose,* shared his insights about the ego in Chapter Three called, "The Core of Ego."

In essence, he described the ego as having two options:

OPTION #1

Superior: higher than another, of greater value . . .

For the ego to maintain superiority, it must keep sending out to others, moment to moment, a communication, either verbally or non-verbally, that they are opposite and being viewed as inferior, poorer, lower in status, and lesser . . .

OPTION #2

Right: morally good, acceptable, justified . . .

For the ego to maintain being right, it must keep intending to others, either verbally or non-verbally, that in some way others are opposite: wrong, don't understand, not performing correctly . . .

The evaluation from the ego is based on judgments, with ego being the judge.

The ego's communication becomes more aggressive when it feels threatened. Often, someone behaves in a way that reminds the ego of a past experience, and it reacts as if threatened again, regardless of the new person or situation. Ego cannot help itself; it is on an autopilot of sorts.

Ego feels there is always something missing. The ego's goal is to maintain relevance—no matter what it takes to hold onto its worth, superiority and rightness—while communicating that others are inferior and wrong.

When operating our lives from a higher perspective, we base our evaluation process on being of value in the situation. For example, someone may be acting in a way that appears angry or disappointed. This is an opportunity to make an indelible impact. *"If they are acting this way, something has happened to cause them to be suffering."* Rather than being annoyed, ask them, *"How is everything going?"* The question alone causes a shift, usually in their condition, when they receive an attitude from someone showing compassion. For example, when taking a client to a restaurant and the waiter is communicating an unpleasant attitude and tone.

Consider adopting a broader attitude that overrides the ego: *"Even though the waiter is offering their service in a lower level of quality than I am accustomed to experiencing, know for sure that regardless of how this appears, everyone is doing their best in this moment."* None of us can know the full story of what is causing the attitude and behaviors. Our attitude of kindness will feel amazing to ourselves and those receiving our compassion. We will carry this energy throughout our day, and others we interact with will feel that energy, as well. Compassion is a magnificent energy!

The most important areas to address are the judgments we hold onto from past hurts, disappointments, cruelties, betrayals, deceit from ones we trusted, theft, infidelities, lies, discrediting, and friends gossiping to provoke harm—just to name a few situations that lead to judgments.

> *You can only lose something that you have, but you cannot lose something that you are."*
> —Eckhart Tolle

Looking at our lives from a higher view, everything happens for a reason: usually for our own benefit and growth. When we look at our disappointments from a higher, broader view, we see each person, event and even betrayal as preparation, not punishment, for our lives to open and our purpose to unfold.

We will naturally evolve into new situations and will organically move away from people and circumstances who no longer contribute to our larger purpose. Learning from these scenarios as neither good nor bad, we begin to understand that all events facilitate a higher purpose. Events that have taken place do not cause suffering. Our judgment of the events causes the suffering.

Letting go of our judgments can be worked out in the exercise provided in Step Three. List the disappointments, the individuals and the situations, and with each one, ask yourself, *"What did I learn from this situation and person? What happened in my life as a result? What have I become because that event happened?"*

This is taking a broader, higher view to more clearly see the bigger picture. When we can see an event from a higher perspective and without judgment, then the energy of judgment releases upon sight, with ease. In that moment, when the energy of judgment and negativity are released, there will be a lighter sense, a breath of fresh air and a freer feeling.

"Some changes look negative on the surface but you will soon realize that space is being created in your life for something new to emerge." — Eckhart Tolle

PRACTICAL APPLICATION

The shifts we make in our evaluation process from the ego-based *"being right"* to the value-based *"being of value"* at first are premeditated, deliberate, ongoing decisions we make from situation to situation. In the moment when someone is judging and criticizing us, possibly in front of others, the choice to strike back and make them wrong is coming from an ego-based premise. Ego is judgment and knows it must win, always.

During a business plan design workshop, an attendee took issue with one of the subjects I offered in the class. Every subject addresses productivity and effectiveness dynamics: what is taking place during productivity, and what is interfering when not productive. The results become the teacher.

An attendee communicated their disapproval in a dramatic way by standing up and holding their arms outstretched as if embracing the other attendees in the room, establishing, *"We all disagree with you on this subject."*

In that moment, even though I easily could have disproved this individual's premise, making them wrong would have been of no value. My value-based intentions provided an interesting question to ponder about the attendees in the class before answering.

"What if this class was interested in observing what it looks like to be judged and criticized, and how to handle it? My sense was they all assumed the only option was to strike back." In that moment, for whatever reason, I realized that this attendee's ego had been threatened and had to re-establish its superiority and rightness by publicly making me wrong and incorrect.

There is no value in reacting to someone who is coming from an ego place. The ego is only interested in being right, being superior and winning at all costs. That is ego's only function. No matter what, there is no conversation or debate available unless one surrenders to ego and engages in a right and superior exchange.

After respectfully listening to what this individual needed to say in full, I chose to respond calmly and in kindness: *"I will not engage with you or anyone where the outcome makes someone wrong."* I said this in a peaceful and non-judgmental manner. The attendees in the room were surprised at my response, and to see that we maintained the peace and creativity in the room. The ego is prepared to fight to win. The value-driven choice was not to fight and not to play along.

Two weeks later, this attendee reached out and wanted to talk and share how much they had learned from our interaction and the impact of my choice not to fight back. The first thing I noticed was this individual looked fifteen years younger than when I saw them in class.

This person had a lightness and a freshness of attitude that was perceptible. Letting go of judgment causes an energy release of significant magnitude.

After sharing their insights into what they learned and their new attitude free of self-righteousness and judgment, I shared, *"That's why you look fifteen years younger! Thank you, and congratulations!"*

The individual added that what woke them up was my intention not to be willing, or not needing, to fight back. I believe the reason the impact was so transformational is that my communication came from the intention of creating a safe place and holding a non-threatening, non-judgmental value-driven attitude. The results proved this outcome was of high value to the class, and an indelible experience for this individual.

Step Three: Judgment

"Some changes look negative on the surface but you will soon realize that space is being created in your life for something new to emerge."
—Eckhart Tolle

_____
_____
_____
_____
_____
_____
_____
_____
_____
_____
_____
_____
_____
_____
_____
_____
_____

"The primary cause of suffering is judgment." —Darylle Virginia Dennis

**Personal – Financial – Professional
Physical – Spiritual**

"A business that is conscious is a group of people that get together for a purpose that is significant for them. The higher levels of consciousness in a company or in a human being is asking, what is my purpose, why am I here, how am I going to contribute to something that is bigger than myself and more enduring. At the highest level of consciousness, business is an act of service."

—Dr. Fred Kofman

step four

IMPACT AWARENESS

ALBERT EINSTEIN

"We know from daily life that we exist for other people first of all, for whose smiles and well-being our own happiness depends."

Awareness of our impact on others with conscious clarity is an essential step in understanding ourselves and our world. This awareness will cause our potential, strengths, gifts, talents, intuition and creativity to emerge with such dynamism that it will take our breath away!

The intention of each teaching from the Value vs. Force Educational Series™ is to illustrate the significance of internal attitudes and external actions, and the dynamics that follow, which set into motion all outcomes and results in our lives. The awareness, in and of itself, begins the journey of understanding that our outcomes are within our grasp to influence.

A course correction on attitudes with matching actions will activate our deeper potential, which consistently results in increased productivity and effectiveness. Our internal dynamics are the first consideration and the most important to address before we perform any activities.

Have you ever thought of yourself as a transmitting tower emitting signals that communicate the totality of your beliefs, attitudes and judgments non-verbally to others? Just like gravity, whether we believe gravity is true or not, gravitational forces are consistently in motion. Whether we believe we are transmitting towers or not, it is a fact that the energy we emit is communicating our state of mind at all times.

Effectiveness and productivity are at the core of each of these teachings, yet the current business education and training centers around the mechanics and actions needed to generate opportunity and wealth. Very little is offered in business education to address how significant and impactful our attitudes and beliefs are, which affect our outcomes in all aspects of our lives.

The education currently offered for business growth strategies addresses the "doing" aspects of management and business development. Rarely, if at all, do they address how we are "being," which matters most. Business flows through people. Opportunity flows through people. Money flows through people.

Impact awareness addresses the aspects of our attitudes, which cause the highest amount of gain or loss. Consider looking at the times we have been impatient and snapped at someone who, in their mind, was doing their best.

Alternatively, think of the times we've been impatient and thanked someone for their efforts to go the extra mile because of our urgency. What is the difference in how we feel? What is the difference in how they act? Becoming aware of our impact on another is the first step in broadening our perspective and experiencing the vastness of our influence.

Two attitudes that cause significant harm are indifference and insensitivity. These attitudes communicate, *"The person or situation doesn't matter . . . worthless."* Our unawareness of having caused harm, most of which is unintentional, still has the potential to weaken, discourage and shame someone to their core.

On the other hand, being aware and conscious of having an impact on every situation and person has a considerable positive influence. At a deeper level, this awareness causes a sincere desire to encourage and uplift those around us, even in the briefest of moments. Once aware of our impact on others, we will be less likely to disregard another and become the cause of their pain.

Behavioral science studies have shown that we, as human beings, are hard-wired to contribute and make a positive difference. Our natural, authentic instincts are to nourish, encourage, support and uplift another. An aspect of our growth will be to become aware that we are impacting others at all times. The quality of our impact on others depends on us.

Any time we act authentically, the encouragement we offer to another triggers a deep sense of peace and fulfillment inside ourselves. The quality of these interactions, and our intentions to be of value to another, has everything to do with our success in business settings. These successes are equivalent to the value created for others.

Dr. Fred Kofman, MIT teacher of the year award recipient in 1992, and author of *Conscious*

Business, shared his views on what being conscious means. During this interview, he said:

"A business that is conscious is a group of people that get together for a purpose that is significant for them. The higher levels of consciousness in a company or in a human being is asking, what is my purpose, why am I here, how am I going to contribute to something that is bigger than myself and more enduring. At the highest level of consciousness, business is an act of service.

"Conscious Business is a business, I dare to say is based on love; based on the Greek notion of Agape; which is a commitment to the welfare and the growth of anybody around me. It's a heart desire to see other people grow, to give them something that's valuable for them, something that will help them and in exchange receive from them the resources that will enable me to thrive and grow and not only survive; but actually live."

Success in business and in life begins with connectivity to others. The quality of the connection with others determines the outcomes of our fulfillment, success and prosperity. Connecting with others triggers our potential, which becomes activated. This is the basis of growth and the development of our character. Our character growth stems from a deeper understanding of those around us and becomes a catalyst for our development in every possible way.

- Intention to be of value for others creates the opportunity for connection.
- Value-driven practices establish the actual connection; therefore, access to others and opportunities to cultivate the relationship.
- The quality of our access generates quality opportunities.

PRACTICAL APPLICATION

One morning, I was getting into an elevator to arrive a bit early for a meeting I had on the sixth floor. The building was small, and the sixth floor was the top level. As the doors began to close, an elderly man was approaching to get into the elevator. I held the doors open and noticed he was hunched over and walking with a cane. He had a tone of tired, angry, disappointed . . . as if he felt like his time here was over.

My intention is to be of value in every moment, and in this situation, I wanted to bring some joy and laughter to the man to lighten his heavy load. I asked, *"Excuse me, Sir, by any chance are you going to the sixth floor?"*

Looking down to the floor, hunched over, he tapped his cane on the floor and said in an annoyed tone, and at the same time as a tap, *"Yes!"* I then said, *"I am so happy to hear this! I hate traveling alone!"*

His reaction was a burst of laughter, he stood up a bit straighter, and I believe he felt I was flirting with him. This made him so happy. The burst of joy exploding inside of him came rushing toward me like a burst of light. I could feel his joy! The elevator doors opened, I held the doors for him to exit, and I went into the office to join my meeting. Much to my surprise, the joy I was feeling from him was radiating from me to the receptionist. She asked if I had just fallen in love. She said, *"You look like a glowing orb!"*

The energy exchanged between each other, even in the briefest of moments, can be electrifying! The meeting went extremely well, as if my joy was being transmitted in some way and changed the entire dynamic of the gathering. This was in a business setting. Remember the goal? Effectiveness and productivity. The brief moment of intending to bring some brightness and value to the elderly man changed my condition to brightness as well. This entire exchange could not have been more than a minute. Much came for us both within that minute. Conclusion: the value of a minute holds the quality of our futures. The value of kindness to another is priceless and eternal.

Step Four: Impact Awareness

"At the highest level of consciousness, business is an act of service."

_____
_____
_____
_____
_____
_____
_____
_____
_____
_____
_____
_____
_____
_____
_____

"A conscious professional holds a heartfelt desire to see people grow and give them value above and beyond income streams."

**Personal – Financial – Professional
Physical – Spiritual**

"The way we understand ourselves and our world is always evolving. From instinct to intuition to intellect, part of being human is using multiple ways to gather and utilize information."

—Institute of Noetic Sciences

step five

ACCESS INTUITIVE INTELLIGENCE

ALBERT EINSTEIN

"The intuitive mind is a sacred gift and the rational mind is a faithful servant. We have created a society that honors the servant and has forgotten the gift."

"*Knowing without knowing how you know*" is a perfect way to describe the aspect of our innate qualities that have *"knowing,"* which is the intuitive dimension of our human design. More likely than not, most of us have had a sense of thinking about someone, and then they call, text or email. Or have you ever said something to someone, and then asked yourself, *"Who said that?"* as they respond with, *"That was just what I needed to hear. Never thought of it like that before. Thank you!"*

People from all over the world share experiences and stories of decisions they suddenly made to change plans without any reason or evidence. Sometime after the fact, they realized their decision was correct for themselves. Dramatic stories are told from those who have avoided natural or otherwise disasters, to then wonder where their decisions came from.

The actor Mark Wahlberg, during an ESPN televised interview, shared his story of buying an airline ticket to go to San Francisco from Boston on September 11, 2001, and he got an overwhelming urge to go to Canada instead. He followed his intuition and changed his plans suddenly.

What if we were able to access Intuitive Intelligence intentionally? How would that affect our professional and personal lives? How efficient would we become with each decision if we were making decisions from an intuitive sense? Imagine building our businesses through *"leading by sensing the future."*

"Every profound innovation is based on an inward-bound journey" is a quote from Otto

Scharmer, co-author of *Presence*. This concept is not a foreign belief in many areas of self-development; however, in business trainings and practices, any concept perceived to have spiritual overtones is not welcomed. Who or what originated the belief that addressing internal dynamics for self-development was earmarked for spirituality alone?

Self-development is what Dr. Abraham Maslow, as a behavior scientist, brought attention to globally, claiming we are born to strive and achieve our highest potential, a deep longing that will not subside. We develop our potentials through ongoing practices of interacting with others, which is one of the greatest gifts the business world offers. The results of interactions with others motivate us to make choices for improving the results, improving ourselves and creating ideas for improving circumstances and situations.

Where do we look when desiring a change or a transformation? Does it matter whether we are working in a bank, or communing with others in a church, as to the path for personal development? For whatever the reason, it appears in business we are only looking to our minds for solutions and ideas. It seems that only in spiritual development do we look internally for growth and deeper understandings. Interestingly enough, we are the same human being whether we are standing in a bank or a church. Why would it be different in either place?

> *"We know a great deal about what leaders do and how they do it. But we know very little about the inner place, the source from which they operate. And it is this source that "Theory U" attempts to explore."*
> —Otto Scharmer in Theory U

For decades, we have said that the New Frontier is an exploration of the deep sea or space exploration. The value of what we learn from space and sea will surely revolutionize life on Earth as we know it today. However, we will not be able to enjoy the quantum leaps that await us if we are not able to keep up with the speed around us; it's ever-changing, ever-accelerating.

The New Frontier and the accessing of Intuitive Intelligence will be a fundamental requirement, and likely the challenges of keeping up will be possible in part to our willingness to explore an inward journey.

The New Frontier is an Inward Journey

We will be able to enjoy the journey in business and life with all its speed when we anchor our dominant operating system in accessing Intuitive Intelligence, which is an internal journey with no limitations regarding speed. Everything we know today is changing at speeds beyond our mind's capacity to comprehend, and it is full speed ahead; there is no turning back now.

The chaos surrounding global societies is due to the impact of the speed at which things are moving and changing. Our ineffectual attempts to evaluate and make decisions on which direction to take, from our minds only, soon will no longer be a viable option. There will be no frame of reference to evaluate directions to take, as the current changes will appear to move at the speed of light.

> *"The way we understand ourselves and our world is always evolving. From instinct to intuition to intellect, part of being human is using multiple ways to gather and utilize information."*
> —Institute of Noetic Sciences

Most athletic competitions provide an example of hyper speed and decision-making. Imagine watching a hockey match, and a player hits the hockey puck, which is now coming directly toward the opposing player. How many thoughts can a player form before making a decision about what to do, before the player is hit in the forehead and lying on the ice? Would we count it in nanoseconds?

Athletes refer to Intuitive Intelligence as being in The Zone. The dominant operating system anchored in The Zone is where Intuitive Intelligence lives. Two wonderful quotes from two athletes say it all:

> *"My legs think faster than I do."*
> —INGEMAR STENMARK, SWEDISH ALPINE SKIING CHAMPION

> *"Skate where the puck's going, not where it's been."*
> —WAYNE GRETSKY, ICE HOCKEY PLAYER

This would be the same in basketball, track and field, volleyball and tennis, to name a few. Have you ever thought that sporting events are opportunities to see what being in The Zone looks and feels like? Are we learning about the value of being in The Zone through our observations of athletes in play, and could Intuitive Intelligence be significant in our futures? Is this an unknown, subconscious, deeper attraction to sports? Do we need to learn this now for our daily lives? Maybe, maybe not; however, accessing this higher intelligence that dwells in the intuitive field is essential for our survival and our ability to thrive in the very near future.

The fact that Intuitive Intelligence is being taught in many countries around the world is an indicator of certain urgency now. MIT Sloan Graduate School of Management, together with other educational institutions around the world, is currently teaching high-profile leaders of Fortune 500 companies that the new management strategy is essential, which is *"Lead by Sensing the Future."* New emerging business leaders of the future are also being prepared to lead from an intuitive position rather than an economic position only.

Ideally, the new model for success is to utilize intuition alongside economics, intuiting the future and economically benefiting. Coherence between intuiting the future as a management strategy, and experiencing economic growth as a byproduct, results in maintaining relevance today and in the future.

WHAT IS NECESSARY TO ACCESS THE INTUITIVE INTELLIGENCE FIELD?

> Oxford English Dictionary definition:
> Intuition: *"the ability to understand or know something immediately, without conscious reasoning."*

According to Albert Einstein, the pathway to connecting with what we want, no matter what it is, is to realize:

"Everything is energy and that's all there is to it! Match the frequency of the reality you want, and you cannot help but get that reality. It can be no other way. This is not philosophy. This is physics."

As unusual as this universal truth may be in a business education course, one may wonder what this has to do with the business world and conducting business? The science of quantum physics, worldwide, continues to study the relationship of our psychological and emotional condition and the impact we collectively have on all results in our world.

Strong evidence exists that we are effecting our outcomes, moment to moment, and the environment responds in a mirror-like manner to our fundamental tone. In other words, the environment is a mirror for our internal state.

Intuitive Intelligence is a higher energetic tone or frequency, similar to radio, which has different frequencies for different stations. Accessing Intuitive Intelligence, according to Oxford English Dictionary, in part, is: *"without conscious reasoning."* Another way to describe accessing this field of intelligence would be heart-based tones, as compared to mind-based evaluations.

Examples of heart-based tones and higher frequencies are:

Gratitude – Love – Joy – Passion – Purposeful – Value Intentions

The mind operates in an evaluation mode, which is analyzing, comparing and judging. As an example, we would not decide to fall in love. Love would be a consequence, an outcome of a quality relationship filled with joy and appreciation. The higher conditions come from heart-based tones. Intentions launched in each moment from higher states are what drive access into Intuitive Intelligence.

Take a moment and observe yourself growing your business with potential new clients or expanding it with existing clients, then apply any of the higher conditions when imagining working with someone.

The intention to be of value to another not only raises our own state of being the moment we interact with another in this state, but our influence also raises their condition to a similar condition as ours. The person with whom you are interacting also is driven to be of value and make a difference. An intent to connect from a value-driven premise activates a similar condition in the other, which is deeply authentic and familiar to both.

Much happens quickly when we operate businesses from higher states. We establish trust unusually quickly when connecting with another holding an intent to be of value. We are all born with a drive to make a difference and make things better or bigger. Intention to be of value to another, or to a situation for the benefit of another, is the applied practice enabling access to Intuitive Intelligence in a moment. Intention to be of value opens access to Intuitive Intelligence. Indescribable energy is now present in our hearts, and our minds are filling up with profound knowing. Creative energy is now abundantly flowing in harmony with the situation launched by the original intention.

The first time you have this experience of accessing the field of Intuitive Intelligence, there will be no doubt this field is available at all times. The results will be extraordinary and will surpass all past business methodologies. You will then have a firsthand experience of *"Knowing without knowing how you know."*

Practical Application

In late October 2007 in Scottsdale, Arizona, a young woman named Gina approached me during the break of a business plan design class I was offering, and wanted to discuss her concerns about the future of the company where she worked. Her concerns indicated that significant challenges were unfolding at her company, and she shared that doubt was spreading as to the business's chance of survival. The business plan design class she attended was such a different approach to any other methodology she had experienced. She thought if she could possibly apply these new ideas in her company, it may have a chance of survival.

Gina set up an appointment for me to make a presentation to the president and director of marketing at her company. At this time in Arizona, an impending market crash was building in the real estate market. Arizona and Nevada were both feeling the impact of a significantly declining market ahead of the rest of the country. Gina worked for a title insurance guaranty company, which depended exclusively on the real estate and mortgage industry for escrow closings and title insurance.

The president of the title insurance guaranty company was leading and managing from an old Industrial Age methodology; numbers were all that mattered. The required actions to bring in the numbers were to see a defined number of people each day. The required volume of people to see would be possible if the sales representatives didn't spend too much time with any one person. Once in front of a potential client, they were to ask for a transaction, and then move quickly to the next potential opportunity.

When companies treat people as merely transactions, the people can easily feel that intention, and frankly, it does not feel welcoming when receiving an attitude from someone who only sees others as a transaction.

Then, for extra challenges, the president used another old methodology to force actions from his sales team. The old method was to threaten the salespeople using the numbers they were required to bring in by a certain date, and if they did not accomplish the goal, they would be let go. Frightening someone who is already alarmed at the market turn will certainly not empower them to go out into the field and inspire businesses to direct transactions to their company.

This was the situation for which Gina had requested help, and it was dire, indeed. The president couldn't be bothered with listening to the formal prepared presentation and made clear his lack of interest by looking out the window and looking at his watch. I stopped the presentation by the second page and closed the folder. Then I said, *"This isn't for everyone, and that's okay. Read the proposal later or not at all. In the meantime, enjoy your Thanksgiving and Christmas."* Then I left.

Gina walked with me to my car and said, *"This isn't over!"* I admired her spirit and commitment to save the company for all the families, as the holidays approached.

Based on what happened next, I later teased Gina by saying, *"God forbid if you should pass away before me; however, if you do, I will go to your gravesite and write on your tombstone, "This isn't over!"*

As a consultant, you know that if you do not have the agreement and support of the governing body of an organization, there is little hope to make a difference. Gina, on the other hand, through her determination, got a reluctant agreement from the president to bring me in again and see what's possible. I agreed exclusively because of the passion of this young salesperson, Gina!

To turn around the weak and ineffective momentum, a course correction of attitude was the first order of the day. People do business with people. The discouragement was apparent with the salespeople, escrow officers, other team members and management of several divisions in the company who dreaded going out and asking for business, and coming back without any business, day in and day out.

Regardless of the market or the fears launched by the president, as well as the uncertainty of the future for all those working in this company, I told them that, "Today will be the first day of the rest of an entirely new future!"

Friday, December 28, 2007 – 8:30 a.m.

This was the first day of launching Value Exchange Dynamics™ – Practical Prosperity Practices. It was also the last business day of the week, month and year.

The room was filled with the sales team, escrow officers, department heads in the Title

Department, the director of marketing, the president and other top executives working directly with the president.

The Value Exchange Dynamics™ business plan design workshop has three fundamental components:

1. Choose who you wish to work with . . .
2. What would be of value above and beyond your income stream?
3. Who else is connected to the same clients for different reasons?

Question One
"Who is your customer?"

Answer
"Real estate and mortgage companies."

***(Question Two deals with the concept of value, which is value offered to the well-being of the client. To sort out a value-driven approach, it was important to find out what was happening with their clients and potential clients in this market.)

Question Two
"What's going on with the real estate agents and mortgage loan officers in both of these markets?"

Answer
"Business has slowed down."

Question Three
"What does that mean then?"

Answer

"Less deals, I guess."

Question Four
"What does that mean then?

Answer
"Less money coming in."

Question Five
"What does that mean then?"

*** (The questions asked were answered by different attendees in the room. They seemed to have a common perception that their clients were merely transactions. The purpose of these questions and answers during the opening of this workshop was for the moment when the people in the room shifted from viewing their clients as transactions, to viewing their clients as human beings.)

Answer
"Maybe some of our clients will have to leave the industry."

Question Six
"What does that mean then?"

There was silence in the room, and the emotions were now coming to the surface. The moment of shift that I was looking for was coming soon . . .

Answer
"They might lose their own homes."

QUESTION SEVEN
"Are any of your clients single mothers?"

Then the shift happened. Their clients were now real human beings on their own, doing their best to get through a rough cycle in business, dealing with fear and lack. Some of the people in the room began to cry. They had not actually ever looked at their clients as people, only transactions, and embracing this awakening now made change possible.

The issues were now in the open, and our next step as a group was to create solutions for the challenges of their clients. Two issues stood out and needed to be addressed immediately for results to be possible.

ISSUE #1
They were discouraged, frightened and in some cases, hopeless.

Attitudes needed to shift immediately. When people are discouraged, frightened and hopeless, they are at their weakest life condition, and with minimal life force energy, they can't accomplish much. The Law of Attraction explains one exception with an understanding that "likeness attracts." Efforts made in a weak, frightened life condition will only be able to attract clients equally weak and frightened. In an emergency, as this company was experiencing, attracting only other clients as weak as themselves would not be a productive contribution to their situation.

Effectiveness stems from the power self-determination brings; only then will we be able to convert efforts into results. The good news about Issue #1 is that each of these lower conditions stems from belief systems, and with support and encouragement, new beliefs will give birth to new hope and confidence.

The marketing efforts for the New Year would be "consultative selling." Consultative selling means meeting with potential and existing clients to explore goals and objectives, issues and concerns. Assisting someone with clarifying their focus is a significant value offered in and of itself.

Holding conversations about their biggest challenge in the past, and their finest hour causing breakthroughs and what that looked like, were incredibly uplifting. Talking about their favorite clients and why they enjoyed their exchanges began to dissolve fear into hope, and hopeless into powerfulness as they remembered their wins.

The vibrant discussions in the room that morning led to many suggestions of value that would restore drive and confidence for the people in their marketplace. Observing the passion and enthusiasm from the people in this room was visible, tangle evidence that *"within our fundamental core identity is a drive to contribute and make a difference."* By building a marketing plan around these intentions, they created results that were nothing short of miraculous.

Tapping into the human drive to make a difference for those at this company changed everything! Self-determination and expectations are powerful. The most expedient means to activate determination is *"Mission-Driven Marketing."* When determination and passionate drives are activated, our deepest potentials will emerge. From that premise, anything is possible.

Issue #2
They needed business plan design and skills training.

The representatives from this title insurance guaranty company, as well as the clients they were calling on, would both benefit from business planning and improved skills.

At that time, I had been offering this business plan design class across the country for close to three years full time; it was the same class as presented in this workbook. The objective was to strengthen the determination and empower those who produce business for the title insurance guaranty company. The productive channels would be through their own sales team and escrow officers, together with the clients with whom they chose to work. If it is possible to be of value to those we serve and to help them create business for themselves, the automatic byproduct is a profound rise in productive results for the company as a whole.

We organized holding one business plan design seminar per week for the first quarter of the year. A local business offered its training room as a contribution to uplift the spirits of the people who were affected by the market turn. The room sat seventy-five to a hundred people. We booked the first business plan design class for their customers to begin on Wednesday, January 2, 2008.

We would also offer the three-hour business plan design class for independent companies as a complimentary educational opportunity for their Team Members and colleagues. The value we brought dramatically raised the levels of effectiveness and productivity for each company client, as part of the "*Mission-Driven Marketing*" concept.

Communication went out on Saturday, with an invitation to attend the three-hour class on Wednesday for whoever wished to launch the New Year in a remarkable way! With very little notice, we had a full house!

On the first day of consulting, the excitement and passion were palpable in the room to the executives who would launch our new approach in the community within the first week of the New Year. The marketing approach became value-driven and to make a difference, as compared to going into the field with fear and dread to ask for business. The creativity was blossoming in the hearts and minds of all those attending this new business plan design and client care launch. The ideas were bouncing off the walls from such excitement and a longing to be of value to people who could use their help now. The results at the end of the first day of our launch with the executive team were beyond anyone's expectation and clearly, one for the record books!

The first day had come to a close. We were collectively on the same mindset, filled with determination and high expectations that together, we would make a significant difference for the existing and new clients. The difference would be in the lives of the team members offering value, as well as in the lives of their new and existing clients. All who participated would never be the same again!

Who knew we had already begun to make that difference, even though no one made marketing calls or attended appointments from 8:30 a.m. to 3:30 p.m. No one was asking for business from anyone during that time. There was no contact with any clients, either. This team, all day, all together, were changing their minds and opening their hearts to contribute to the well-being of others as a business-building methodology. Everyone could feel the excitement!

We ended the day at 3:30 p.m., and by the time I returned home, it was 4:35 p.m. and I checked my email. Much to my surprise, I received an email from the president of this company, writing, *"It's like a miracle. Today, we had our number one open order count, higher than ever before in our 10-year history! Today!"*

How was it possible to effect this record-breaking result day when the only effort made was in changing attitudes, without any actual effort toward receiving? The effort made here was an internal shift, and the shift was a determination and passion to be of value to those existing and potential clients struggling in a market crisis. Would value-driven practices actually be that effective despite minimal or no effort?

The answer, in part, to *"How was this possible without direct effort?"* would be to consider looking at the results in a business setting through the eyes of quantum mechanics, supported by innumerable global studies on the subject of collective intention and resonance.

Beginning in 2004, quantum physicists began to share with the general public, worldwide, the extraordinary potential we have as human beings to impact and effect our outcomes as individuals. This was when we began hearing expressions go viral like, *"What you think about, you bring about." "How you feel makes things happen faster." "What we put our attention on, grows."*

The Law of Attraction had been offered in seminars and workshops in the early 1990s and went viral globally when this concept was introduced in the book and DVD called *The Secret*. This was when we began to raise our understanding of ourselves as responsible participants in our daily experiences.

Many began to ponder and absorb this new introduction to untapped human potential. Many people in many countries began to practice and apply a management, of sorts, of thoughts and actions exploring if it is true that we are effecting the outcomes of our experiences. Once our attention began to observe patterns and matches from our attitudes resulting in outcomes, then we truly began to realize we are so much more than we've been taught.

A new normal began to spread in the lives of many people around the world. The new journey was to learn how to intentionally create opportunities, and this intention begins with an internal combination of visualizing the results, in a movie-like manner, as if they have been attained now. At the same time as the movie-like visualization and seeing the result of the desired goal, the individual opens a deep gratitude for what they desired and what is now existing in their daily experience. Results appear in perfect harmony with the original intention, void of any unnecessary strategies or volume of actions.

This new discovery, now proven true in daily life, has opened the doors to an acceleration of an even greater experience.

An acceleration of the individual experience is a collective experience of visualization, and a collective appreciation for the desired result, also referred to as resonance—a collective resonance experience. Here's a dictionary definition of resonance: *"to continue to have a powerful effect or value."*

Currently, studies are conducted around the world, observing the results from group intentions. A dictionary definition of intention, in part, means: *"quality of purposefulness."* A group holding collective intentions and qualities of purposefulness launches a powerful intention, generating geometric progressions and quantum leaps. The accompanying results occur without actions taken.

On December 28, 2007, the executive team of the title insurance company, without realizing the power the change of hearts and minds toward their clients would have, actually effected a collective resonance that went into the real estate community like a beautiful song. Whoever was doing new business in real estate on the last working day of the year, and required escrow and title services, for reasons of resonance, this company was the one that came to mind to many on that day!

The outside environment will always respond to the signals we emit from our state of mind, beliefs and judgments that we hold as truths. We can override a lower condition of life by activating an intention to be of value and serve others. When intending value for another, the actions that we take come from an inspired place, as compared to a *"must do"* place. There is no comparison to the benefits that result in a value-driven business practice to a business practice filled with strategies of doing for the sake of needing to do.

A public relations professional in a Scottsdale mortgage company wrote and published in an article, *"This title company is the only voice of hope in Maricopa County."* (The name of the title company was included in the article.)

This was a tremendous experience that revealed the power of The New Journey as an Internal exploration, after all. There is much power and magnificence inside each one of us. Let's go inside first and create what's possible! All actions will be inspired and organically self-organized flawlessly for each situation and person! Unstoppable!

> "Someday after mastering the winds, the waves, the tides and gravity, we shall harness the energies of love, and then for a second time in the history of the world, man will have discovered fire."
> —Pierre Teilhard de Chardin

Bonus Experience

At the beginning of the practical application experience story, I mentioned a brilliant young woman named Gina, who was responsible for bringing this teaching into her company. Gina and I have stayed in touch, and each time we speak or meet, it always feels like we connected as recently as yesterday, even though it may have been months or years.

Gina and I shared an amazing experience, encouraging, uplifting and being of value to a depressed community of realtors and mortgage agents, not to mention the title insurance guaranty company, with its management and staff knowing their future was fragile.

One morning, well before the sun had risen, when there was quiet, peacefulness and creativity, something occurred to me that seemed like a wonderful idea and contribution to this teaching and workbook. Gina came to mind so powerfully that I felt an excitement about exploring with her if she would be open to sharing her experience from her point of view. After all, she was there! She always referred to the unfolding benefits coming to so many during this consulting project as being a *"witness to miracles."*

Gina agreed and has written her testimony from her recall and experience, which may benefit others who are considering a new way to *be* in business.

Here's Gina!

"I witnessed a miracle in January 2008. I was a sales executive at the time for a title guaranty company in Arizona. It was a grim time in real estate. I had been in the title insurance business since 2003, and had never seen or felt the despair from my realtor clients like I had witnessed in 2007/2008. I knew our company was struggling, and I was very worried about the future for my company and the families of each of our team members, and worried about their future so close to the holidays.

I had met Darylle Virginia Dennis in October 2007 at one of her business plan design events. I loved her methodologies, and it gave me hope for our company, as well as my realtor and lender clients. I was determined to get her in front of our clients! With more than expected prompting and a significant degree of pushback, finally an agreement was reached for Darylle to roll out our first client care meeting in January 2008. Darylle would bring to our clients and our team the business plan design event I had seen and experienced in October 2007.

I will remember that day for the rest of my life. Most of the people entered the room that morning with little hope. This was a time when foreclosures and short sales were now the new normal. One of my favorite clients at the time was a very successful realtor who had become "Rookie of the Year" with his company in 2005. He had hit an all-time low in the middle of 2007. He sat front-row center that morning with his wife, who was also a realtor.

By the end of the meeting, his posturing had changed and he seemed to have made a shift. I set up a meeting for him and his wife to meet with Darylle right after the class. After a one-hour private meeting, he was filled with hope and high expectations.

One week later, at the second client care meeting, he stood up in front of everyone and shared that he had applied what he learned from Darylle Virginia Dennis, and approached his business completely differently.

He was now leading with value and asking his clients if they would like to explore building an opportunity together, and where he may be of value. He was no longer asking for business, rather, asking to be of value to them. It was as if his business had changed overnight. Within eighteen days, he had contracts on five transactions in the higher, more exclusive areas of Scottsdale.

Unexpectedly, he opened his escrow and title insurance transactions with us. The astounding part of this experience is the market was still significantly challenged. Foreclosures were the daily normal, and the only thing that changed was his attitude and his high expectations for success with a business plan to be of highest value.

He was one of many clients who had shared amazing success stories every week. As a company, we were hitting record numbers as well. Darylle Virginia Dennis is a miracle worker. She has a way of delivering the message in a way that you can apply what you learn immediately, and it will change your life!"

STEP FIVE: ACCESS INTUITIVE INTELLIGENCE

"Knowing without knowing how you know." —Dean Radin, PhD

_____
_____
_____
_____
_____
_____
_____
_____
_____
_____
_____
_____
_____
_____
_____
_____

"The intuitive mind is a sacred gift…"
—Albert Einstein

**PERSONAL – FINANCIAL – PROFESSIONAL
PHYSICAL – SPIRITUAL**

"The words gratitude and love form the fundamental principles of the laws of nature and the phenomenon of life. By contrast, words such as, "You Fool" do not exist in nature and are instead unnatural elements created by people. Words that revile, harm, and ridicule are results of the culture created by humans."

—Dr. Emoto

step six

GRATITUDE

SRI BHAGAVAN

"The universe is structured to naturally respond to the needs and desires of a grateful individual. It is only a person with gratitude who can hold a vision and lead it to completion since his brain and nervous system are wired differently."

A familiar quote that went viral some time ago, and people still share it to this day, is this: *"Have an Attitude of Gratitude."* Oprah, speaking on her talk show early on, encouraged audiences to awaken to the value of keeping a Gratitude Journal, each day writing about things to be grateful for in their lives. Gratitude Journals now are considered a practice for many people, similar to setting goals. Making lists of things we want, appreciation for things we have, and intending to accomplish a tangible result, all lead to a positive state of mind.

There is much more to it than making lists and writing what we want and appreciating what we have. Many have approached goal setting by thinking about what they want and writing it down. Years of writing lists of goals and not receiving satisfactory results eventually leads to developing a belief system that goal setting does not work. Setting goals and objectives does work and is incredibly powerful when approached with a deeper understanding of the dynamics present to produce a result. Then anything is possible.

To produce a desired goal is an alignment process, not a decision-making process. Actually, the objective is to manifest and receive goals. The desired outcome will happen every time we are in vibrational alignment to the desired result. We cannot desire money and feel at the same time *"that will never happen for me"* and expect the desired result of money to appear. The frequency of receiving money and the frequency of *"that will never happen for me"* are not congruent. Our power source for alignment is a heart-based connection process. This is something we feel, not something we think.

The same holds true for gratitude. Gratitude is a state of being, not an attainment. Choosing what to be grateful for is a decision, not a state of being. Being happy is a state of being. Being abundant is a state of being. Being in love is a state of being. Imagine deciding to set a goal to fall in love today and be done by 5:15 p.m. That would sound quite ludicrous.

All of these states of being are readily available when connecting from a heart-based point of origination. The benefits of being in a state of gratitude are considerable.

Dr. Masaru Emoto was a Japanese scientist who brought to global consciousness, as a result of thousands of studies, the concept that our thoughts and intentions have a definitive impact on the physical world. Dr. Emoto's studies included scientific evidence of the molecular structure of water molecules transforming once exposed to intentions, thoughts and sounds.

In Dr. Emoto's book, *Hidden Messages in Water*, he validates, through case studies, that the power of our intentions does, in fact, result in the alteration of the molecular structure of water in a mirror-like manner, matching the intention launched. The shape of the molecules showed changes of beautiful, hexagonal crystal shapes when exposed to positive intentions. In contrast, negative intentions exposed incomplete, asymmetrical patterns appearing to look similar to the implosion and collapse of the molecular structure.

What took the world by storm was the eventual result of his case studies, which demonstrated the most influential state of being we embody as humans is the state of gratitude.

In *Hidden Messages in Water*, Dr. Emoto writes, *"The words gratitude and love form the fundamental principles of the laws of nature and the phenomenon of life. Therefore, water in its natural form is required to create the hexagonal form. By contrast, words such as, "You Fool" do not exist in nature and are instead unnatural elements created by people. Words that revile, harm, and ridicule are results of the culture created by humans."*

Living in societies where competition is fierce and maintaining relevance is a daily aim, negativity and judgments can easily seep into our emotional states, which are all byproducts of fear. If water molecules show harmony with *nature and the phenomenon of life,* and our bodies are 75 percent water, imagine what is happening to our bodies and our emotional states when we are negative toward ourselves or others. According to Dr. Emoto's studies with water, negativity is not in harmony with nature, and by thousands of results from his studies, negativity of any form causes an effect on the water molecules of implosion and deformation.

This is a new era of conscious awakening of our value and significance. When we are able to stay in a high state of gratitude, hold clarity of our value, and clarity of the value of others and life itself, it will evoke a lightness of being and a profound realization of how magnificent it truly is to be alive in this world.

Here's the Oxford English Dictionary definition of gratitude:

"Quality of being thankful; readiness to show appreciation for and to return kindness."

Additional definitions of gratitude: *"See the nature of; increase the value of; absence of resistance; absence of everything that feels bad."*

Gratitude is the highest state we embody. Dr. Emoto repeatedly showed in studies that gratitude is the most positive influential state we have available. When we are in a state of gratitude, everything works out for our best interest organically. Goodness surrounds those in a grateful state. Gratitude heals judgments held from a long-ago past or from current disappointments. A state of gratitude opens access to creativity and solutions for circumstances impacting our lower states.

Accessing Intuitive Intelligence, as shown in Step Five, is possible when first understanding Intuitive Intelligence as higher vibrational tones and frequencies. One of the highest frequencies enabling access to align with Intuitive Intelligence is gratitude. There are infinite possibilities available when creating new and more from higher vibrational tones. Gratitude is the highest of vibrational tones.

A shift is taking place globally, that in part, is an evolution and a new awareness of our potentials. We are all so much more than we have been taught. Our emerging potentials are simultaneously facing challenges we have not ever faced before in human history. First of all, the speed at which information is proliferating is significantly beyond our mind's capacity to evaluate and make decisions. The stresses within the hearts and minds of people throughout the world are reaching disturbing levels, without any apparent solutions available.

Know this for sure: solutions exist, and the solutions are as remarkable, extraordinary and astonishing as is the remarkable technology changing life on planet Earth as we know it today.

As individuals, our journey is inward. Remember, the New Frontier is an Inward Journey.

One of the channels to enter the higher-self, the genius and creative you that enables a connection with Intuitive Intelligence, is gratitude!

To repeat the quote by Sri Bhagavan at the beginning of this chapter:

"The universe is structured to naturally respond to the needs and desires of a grateful individual. It is only a person with gratitude who can hold a vision and lead it to completion since his brain and nervous system are wired differently."

Take a look inside and see through eyes of gratitude for ALL of our experiences, and realize everything has happened for a reason of preparation for this time on Earth. Every experience was essential for depth and growth, and was not an accident or a coincidence. Each event, without one exception, has prepared us for this very time, which will require our full potential to emerge. Then, we can offer our gifts and talents for the value and benefit of others. Gratitude for all of our experiences will be the liberation from lack, limitations and any misguided interpretation of our worthiness. Only now, improving the quality of life in society is possible.

Ideally, gratitude is a continuum flow of appreciation for the kindnesses and generosities offered, then responded to with return acts of gratitude and kindnesses.

When we become conscious of the energy flows between people, and the quality of gratitude as an energy, we begin to experience quantum leaps in the benefits of goodness flooding our lives, in all aspects—personal, financial, professional, physical and spiritual.

∞

A significant area for improvement, perfectly suited for gratitude to flourish and one that will be a powerful witness to astounding results, is the power of gratitude within our corporations.

There is no need to look very far to find example after example of corporations viewing their staff and management through the eyes and behaviors of materialism. A coinciding shift is happening in our corporations, similar to what is globally shifting in societies.

Corporations of all types and industries have much to gain or lose should they take risks and change how they operate in every aspect of their interactions with management, staff and clients. Peter Senge, co-author of *Presence* and senior lecturer at the MIT Sloan Graduate School of Management, wrote brilliantly about the significant challenges facing corporations today. What we need to take place with a sense of urgency is to shift from Industrial Age methodologies to current Global Age methodologies.

The GDP in the USA is 80 percent dominated by service industries; manufacturing is 12 percent of the GDP. Senge eloquently raised the issue that corporate America continues to utilize old Industrial Age methodologies in service-based industries. The Industrial Age was the age of making material things: cars, refrigerators, furniture, tools and much more. Service industries are defined by serving people. Success in service industries originates from quality relationships with clients, management and staff.

Clearly stated, building a car is not the same methodology as building a relationship. The Industrial Age Revolution began in 1755 in London. The industrial leaders implemented strategies and practices for purposes of control. Systemization, predictability and control are efficient means to build materials. These methodologies have limited, at best, productive, effective results and outcomes in service-based companies.

In Senge's co-authored book, *Presence*, he writes about five fundamental characteristics of the Industrial Age. They are: control – predictability – standardization – faster is better – profit.

Let's take each of these Industrial Age characteristics and apply them one at a time to building a service-based company, where quality relationships are key.

- Control – When building a healthy, productive relationship, does the word control come to mind? How would it feel to be controlled by another person? How would it feel to attempt to control another person? The words frustration, belittling and obedience come to mind.

- Predictability – When building a healthy, productive relationship, how likely would it be to predict another person's behavior or predict another person's attitudes or state of mind? Attempting to predict another's attitude and behavior would result in a repeated failure of objectives. Even so, systems are in place today with management policies to control behavior so predictability is possible.

- Standardization – Imagine building a healthy, productive relationship with a person and regulating their behavior and thoughts. Standardization is a *"one-size-fits-all"* communication. This form of communication in a business setting includes companies that utilize scripts for connecting and interacting with others. There are scripts for introducing services, and scripts for overcoming objections should someone decide not to buy the service. Actually, it would be inappropriate to refer to this communication approach as communication.

- Faster is better – This is the most challenging characteristic for relationship-building when applying this particular Industrial Age method in service-based industries. In Industrial Age manufacturing procedures, faster is better for obvious reasons. The faster something is made, the more money it will generate. Painfully obvious to many in relationship-building enterprises is that the "faster is better" strategy is a setup to fail. *"Hurry, buy my program." "Hurry and like me; I have six more calls to make." "I have to make fifteen calls a day; do you like me yet?" "Do you have an idea of when?"* These examples may not be the actual verbal communication; however, they reflect the non-verbal communication, which is ineffective and unproductive.

- Profit – Materials were built and sold, period; no relationship required. The Industrial Age changed the quality of life as it was then known across the world. This was a significant age we continue to benefit from today. Inventing, manufacturing and selling did not require building relationships, and the objective was to make a profit. Relationship-building approaches require quality connections with others. Imagine how it would feel to be approached by someone only interested in connecting because of the profit they could make for themselves. This final Industrial Age characteristic, which is still applied today, is diminishing in its effectiveness.

The book *The Meaning Revolution* by MIT Teacher of the Year recipient (in economics) Fred Kofman, PhD, states this:

"Transcendent leadership has little to do with education or training. Kofman soon discovered that the tools of economics just didn't work in motivating employees. Material incentives account for perhaps 15 percent of employee motivation. The other 85 percent is driven by our need to belong—by the conviction that what we do day in and day out matters."

However, the training and development using Industrial Age methods, in a service age, continues in many companies and industries across the country. Management is still educating and training in old methods, strategies and practices, which take volumes of effort to secure speedy results.

Firms of Endearment author Raj Sisodia wrote, *"Cultural shifts are taking place in the workforce environments. People want to view their work as a calling, something that answers to a higher need. This is transforming the marketplace, the workplace and the very soul of capitalism."*

Many CEOs have this question: *"Why would this be happening at this time? As a CEO, how would I accommodate the "higher needs and infuse a calling for the people who work with this company?" "How would having a calling effect productive outcomes?"*

When management and co-workers view people in the workforce as human beings requiring quality relationships for interactivity and growth, the journey has then begun that answers the question, *"How would I accommodate the higher needs and infuse a calling?"* The shift of culture that is needed now allows for a productive, healthy and creative organization. This begins with respect and appreciation for those contributing their energy, focus and qualities to the organization. Gratitude will profoundly impact the quality and excellence in all aspects of the organization. The employees will return their gratitude to those offering their respect and appreciation by bringing forth their higher potentials as a thank you in return. Gratitude will produce energy and creativity, which will lead to thriving outcomes, and all will benefit greatly.

The first necessary upgrade is to shift from beliefs and attitudes that human beings only represent transactions. Then, shift to attitudes and practices that human beings represent growth, development, creativity, prosperity and expansion. Thriving in all aspects within an organization depends on the caliber, quality and integrity of the people who were hired, and it depends on the gratitude for their presence.

This leads to the second necessary upgrade for a thriving organization: gratitude offered is a way of being. Gratitude is communicated through actions of appreciation. Upper and middle management, on through to the frontline staff, are all human beings who bring a more full, committed potential to their work when they feel appreciated.

Clients share with others their experiences with companies who treat them with gratitude and appreciation. The word spreads, and referrals pour in to those companies who are naturally grateful and exhibit their appreciation with their actions. All people want to be heard, understood and appreciated. When there is discord between people, one, two or all three of these connections are missing. Restore these three connections with communication, and all will be well.

The third upgrade to consider is the quality of our gratitude. Take a bit of a leap and think in terms of parenting a child, teenager or young adult who has been impacted by receiving money as the only means of receiving love. Gifts, cars and allowances offered as a replacement for love from parents who are very busy in a competitive world will be interpreted as being unloved and devalued. The usage of material love will never come close to the power of connection and appreciation for those in our lives. No matter how much money one spends, it will never be enough to replace true connectivity. There is little difference in the workplace with our clients. Do we show our gratitude for their business with money, materials and gifts?

Dr. Emoto's case studies have proven the power of gratitude and its influence on outcomes. The quality of our sincere appreciation is integral for those who collectively determine the quality of our life. Gratitude expressed for everyone who contributes to the quality of our life is essential to realize these are precious and priceless relationships. When we express our gratitude in ways that show our interest and participation in our clients' wellness, it is the finest and most enduring type of gratitude.

A global movement is now increasing in momentum, and it is value-driven education that contributes to the wellness, development and growth of all those around us.

Our family members equate love and appreciation with our participation in their lives and their development. There is little difference between the people who work and build in our organizations. With our actions, the value-driven contribution to each member of the organization is saying, *"We appreciate you and see your potential, which is significant. Let's explore what developing your potential would look like."* The gratitude action returned by the employee, manager or leader communicating their gratitude would naturally be their committed best every day by saying with their actions, *"Thank you for caring about me and seeing my potential that you deem valuable. I love working here!"*

The previous example speaks to employees filled with gratitude each day, communicating their gratitude for their company non-verbally, while taking care of their company's clients. The clients will feel the employees' appreciation for the company they entrusted their business with, and the clients will have an intuitive knowing, *"We made a great choice."*

One of the highest practices and actions in business is to communicate gratitude and appreciate those managers and frontline staff who interact every day with your clients. Educating staff, management and clients supports growth, encouragement and, most of all, participation in their lives. This communicates that they are valued, as are your customers! Repeat business and flows of referrals from happy customers will become a new normal for business growth.

Consulting to commercial banks for five years was a tremendous education through actual experience in ways I could only deem as priceless. After five years of consulting, it was becoming clear that my results for my bank clients were diminishing approximately 10 percent a year. I realized that only teaching was not enough to sustain my value for my clients. The world was moving so fast that it became mandatory for me to get back out in the marketplace as a salesperson to find out what was happening.

The title insurance industry was perfect for my new educational and experiential goals. The title industry works with banks, credit unions, mortgage lending firms, builders and real estate—for the most part, the movers and shakers within any city and state. I was grateful to be hired on the spot and given a higher-end, highly competitive territory where the competition was fierce.

This opportunity was the exact ideal model to sort out what was happening in the business communities and what it would take to catch up and win!

My sales approach was to meet with the owners and bring value to their organizations in a consultative-selling manner. It turns out that my approach was unique to this industry, where the methodology was a volume of calls and how to effect and receive immediate results. It was considered normal to spend huge sums of money to *"buy clients"* through entertaining, trips, box seats at ball games, paid vacations, office upgrades with equipment, furnishings, carpeting and gifts. My head was spinning. Had the business world changed that much in my brief five years of consulting?

The sensibilities I held as a person included a strong desire to be successful because it made good business sense to work with me. I wanted no favors, so I would know at the end of my life that I was successful because of the value I brought to my clients. Gifts and payoffs seemed like cheating. If someone's value isn't enough, let's add money to compensate for the lack of value. Is that the strategy? I wasn't interested in wins that required cheating. By the way, those types of inducements were and still are illegal.

I continued to take excellent care of my clients and went above and beyond, helping grow their businesses through introductions to potential opportunities.

For two years, I had a wonderful mortgage company client who was very loyal. Loyalty was a rare phenomenon in that industry. Daily, competitor companies with new salespeople

Practical Application

were showing up with the next new, shiny object. I occasionally referred to the title industry as *"last seen loyalty."* My routine was dropping by this client's office daily to be available for something of value for their business. Sometimes, something simple was of high value, such as taking a document across town for the closing of a transaction late on a Friday. I was always happy to accommodate.

An incident was about to happen that would teach me a lifelong lesson about gratitude and how significant it is and always will be in a business setting, and of course, in life.

Like clockwork, I entered the office each morning. One morning, the president of the mortgage company had her hand on top of a stack of files she was about to open for title insurance. She said, *"What you say next will determine how many of these files you get today."* Confused by the comment, I asked for clarification. She said, *"Mr. Baker from a title company came in last evening and said that if we showed him the same loyalty we show you, he would be sending my business partner, myself and our husbands on a cruise to Europe."*

Frankly, I was appalled. Are these women asking for a bribe, a payoff for their continued loyalty? I responded angrily, *"Who do you think I am? Five deals you get a toaster and ten deals you get a bicycle? Are you kidding me with this? Give it all to Mr. Baker."* Then I left.

For the rest of the day, I complained to myself about these women asking for a payoff, when I had done so much for them. I had brought them business. I had driven on Fridays in horrific traffic to deliver documents so they could close on Monday. I was there every single day, and many times twice a day. On and on and on went my complaining.

The next morning, in preparing for the day, one of my rituals was meditation time to get my head clear for the day and launch productive, positive intentions. Quieting the mind is incredibly valuable to the quality of each day. Much to my surprise, in the quiet of my mind, a flood of clarity came pouring in about the situation with my clients and their mortgage company.

The extent of my arrogance and lack of gratitude for their loyalty were shown to me in such clarity, like a movie. Suddenly, I could see every day, the volume of people coming into their office asking for their title business, and they continued to say, "No, thank you, we're loyal to Darylle." Day in and day out for weeks, months and now just over two years, they still remain loyal, regardless of the magnitude of efforts and offers to get their business. I had taken them for granted and viewed my extra efforts as a sufficient payback for their loyalty.

Also, I was clearly shown that had I conveyed a sincere appreciation for their business and their remarkable loyalty, the European cruise Mr. Baker was offering would not have even made any difference. The most outstanding realization of all was a profound knowing that when people make a relationship about money, it is an attempt to get someone's attention. *"Do you hear me now?"* What I learned from this experience would change me forever and was a most profound gift from these women. I felt shame and gratitude at the same time. I vowed first thing that morning, I would correct the mess I had made the day before.

I went into their office and asked both women if I could speak with them. Hesitantly, they agreed. I apologized for my attitude and actions the day before and shared that in this morning's meditation, I could clearly see that I had not shown them the gratitude they so richly deserved. Continuing, I shared my realization of their efforts, day in and day out, to fend off immeasurable, unimaginable attempts by others to win their business. The loyalty they had graced me with was deserving of high gratitude. I apologized deeply and sincerely.

Then, I shared, *"What I have learned from this experience has changed my life forever in invaluable ways. To show my gratitude from this precious gift of what I have learned from you, I will continue to come in every day and be of value to you as I have for the last two years. I am not asking for you to continue using my title company. I will deliver documents, even if from Mr. Baker's title company, as my gratitude for what I have learned that will affect the quality of my life for the balance of my life."*

What I never considered or even expected was for these women to continue to entrust all of their title business to my title company. They turned down Mr. Baker's offer of the European cruise, and nothing more was said. I held in my heart a deep gratitude for their loyalty and the gift of appreciation I had learned from them. Their remarkable and continual efforts established the quality of my life. Gratitude made all the difference, with long-standing benefits of appreciation to all the clients who came after this experience. I will remember with affection and depth the profound lesson of a lifetime I received from these incredible women.

STEP SIX: GRATITUDE

"We know from daily life that we exist for other people first of all, for whose smiles and well-being our own happiness depends." —ALBERT EINSTEIN

_____
_____
_____
_____
_____
_____
_____
_____
_____
_____
_____
_____
_____
_____

*"It is only a person with gratitude who can hold
a vision and lead it to completion."*
—SRI BHAGAVAN

**PERSONAL – FINANCIAL – PROFESSIONAL
PHYSICAL – SPIRITUAL**

"Creativity is just connecting things. When you ask creative people how they did something, they feel a little guilty because they didn't really do it, they just saw something."

—STEVEN JOBS

step seven

VISUALIZE

REMEZ SASSON

"The creative power of imagination has an important role in the achievement of success in any field. What we imagine with faith and feelings comes into being. It is the important ingredient of creative visualization, positive thinking and affirmations."

A documentary on the subject of genius was recently shown as a fascinating exploration of where genius comes from and how geniuses think. The interviewer of the program opened by asking an astral physicist, *"How do geniuses think?"*

The astral physicist answered, *"When Albert Einstein was asked a similar question, his response was physicists think in terms of pictures. Albert Einstein referred to his meditative times to 'see' as thought exercises."*

Nikola Tesla began to hold intentions as a small child, and he continued this practice throughout his lifetime. It would contribute to the quality of life on Earth. Tesla's tool of visualizing to create new and more quality for the human race opened an enormous field of intelligence, and he *saw,* in his imagination, pictures of things not yet existing on Earth: words traveling through the air, for example, which became the radio.

Steven Jobs said, *"Creativity is just connecting things. When you ask creative people how they did something, they feel a little guilty because they didn't really do it, they just saw something."*

These three men of science all shared a commonality: they each utilized visualization as a tool, and as a result of what they *"saw,"* each changed the quality of life on planet Earth as we know it today.

"A rising tide lifts all boats" is an ideal way to describe this aspect of goal receiving. The evidence is clear by results, over time, how much our world and our lives have changed and improved, beginning with the dreams and visualizations of the three men mentioned earlier.

Each one of us dreams in our own way of having a quality of life better than where we were at the moment of the new dream. This is in our human nature to continue to make things better and more, continually raising the quality of our own experiences. We don't finish third grade and say, *"Thank you. I'm good now."* We learn, and then we have a thirst for more learning. We experience, and we have a hunger for more experiences. We spend our potential in any given situation and then have an appetite for more potential to emerge.

Being motivated toward improving on all levels of life is the trigger that brings out our potential, which exists in our DNA to become *"self-fully realized."*

The key to bringing the invisible into the visible begins with visualization. Seeing with clarity, including details, causes circumstances and events to bring the visual into reality. The mind cannot distinguish between what it sees in our imagination or what it sees that has already manifested. To the mind, there is no difference.

Visualization is like being in a movie. Getting creative while *"watching your movie in your mind"* would be watching as if you are already living the dream you are visualizing. What are the details, the colors, the environment? Seeing a picture in our mind begins the process of manifesting the result.

For more than twenty-five years, Heartmath Institute has studied and documented how the power of our influence on outcomes exists in how we feel. We cannot think and visualize something we want, and then have our feeling contradict the picture, and expect a successful outcome. Our mind's eye and our heart-based feelings, when in coherence, are the combination that unlocks our ability to receive.

This is the area in which many have developed the concept that goal setting does not work. When we are not receiving the goals we established, what usually is not working is our ability to receive them.

If we are not receiving what we want, we have more doubt and lack in our feelings about receiving the goal than we have expectations to receive.

We can view the results as *"a picture is worth a thousand words."* If the results show outcomes of not receiving what we want, there is more skepticism than expectancy. Once we are aware of our doubts, we need to shift our attention to what we want and focus on our thoughts, subjects, activities and people that activate positive energy.

All negativity is based in fear. As we are creating new and more, fear-based thoughts and negative people will be of no value of any form to accomplish what we want. Move toward thoughts, subjects, activities and people that activate a positive reaction. Move away from any and all negativity. Stay immersed in looking through a mode of receiving, a mode of expectation.

Another aspect to consider during goal receiving cycles is the default mechanism of the mind. When the mind has no information or evidence that our goal is within reach, the mind tends to default toward doubt and negativity.

A simple example is when someone does not return our call. What are we automatically thinking? *"They probably found someone else to work with!"* This evaluation comes without any evidence to support our reasoning for the lack of a returned call. Why do we make up *"truths"* without any information to verify or validate the *"truth"* we now believe is true? These *"truths"* without evidence of any form are coming from our minds, due to the mind's default mechanism of negativity when evidence isn't available.

Then, if our minds are going to make up truth, why would it be necessary to accept loss and failure as truth? Why are we not choosing to guide the mind's eye on the side of our victory? If we are making it up anyway, let's make up good results and good justifiable *"truths." "What we put our attention on expands."* The mind cannot distinguish between what it sees in the mind or what it sees in reality; both are real to the mind.

Our minds can be changed and managed, which will require discipline and focus. *"What we place our attention on grows."* Despite the autopilot of the mind toward negativity when lacking information, once we are aware of this, we can make different choices.

The most substantial catalyst to allowing in what we want, with speed, is maintaining high energy and an excited, passionate life condition. Picturing and feeling the goal as real in our experience, together with an expectation, is a powerful focus and will automatically no longer allow negativity.

Once we have accomplished from our thoughts and dreams, those dreams can become a reality for ourselves, as they did for Roger Bannister, Albert Einstein, Nikola Tesla and Steven Jobs. And then it's so much easier for all future generations to excel and create!

This is the truest definition of *"a rising tide lifts all boats."*

As each one of us establishes goals and dreams, our visualizations will bring those dreams into reality. Then, we will *"be a rising tide."*

Practical Application

Living in Arizona for a short while and having begun my speaking and consulting career, I was interested in purchasing a home. A friend referred me to a beautiful townhouse that had just come onto the market. The new home was the builder's model with all the upgrades one can imagine for a beautiful home. With the cabinets, the fixtures, a magnificent kitchen and stunning landscaping—I knew I had to have this home! On a Monday, four days before going into escrow, the lender called and said, *"We're going to need an additional amount of money. We have until Thursday."*

The real estate market at that time was strong, and it was obvious to all that we were in an escalating fever pitch to buy real estate. As a result, there were many backup buyers for this property. The amount required was beyond my reach at that time, and by all the normal standards, it would not be possible for me to raise that kind of money in four days.

Enter visualization! Many times, I had applied the concept of making a movie as a visualization process. This process works as long as what I see in the movie is in harmony with my feelings about owning this home. I began to see myself standing in this beautiful kitchen, looking out the window at the stunning landscaping in the backyard. I was making the greatest breakfast burrito in the history of food, while basking in every moment I was in this kitchen and lovely home.

Right away, on Monday, I started receiving calls from people in other states where I had offered seminars in the recent past. Those who called were interested in coaching. By the end of Monday, several people had signed up for coaching.

Monday evening and Tuesday morning, I again, in my movie, visualized myself in the kitchen of this beautiful home, looking out the window at the stunning landscaping, making the greatest breakfast burrito in the history of food. On Tuesday, again, calls came in from people in different states, asking about coaching. Three people signed up for coaching, and I now had surpassed the number of dollars I needed by Thursday. On Wednesday, more calls continued to come in, asking about speaking and coaching. Two more people signed up, and I was amazed at the momentum launched from three visualizations, and that I was living in a movie.

This is a powerful process, and each time we live our dream in our visualizations, now made real, we raise the tide for others. The key and the work on our part is the harmony with our mind and heart being in unity.

What do you think was the first thing I did when moving into this beautiful home? Yes, that's right. I made the greatest breakfast burrito in the history of food, and it was delicious on many levels!

STEP SEVEN: VISUALIZE

"What we imagine with faith and feelings comes into being."
—REMEZ SASSON

___
___
___
___
___
___
___
___
___
___
___
___
___
___
___
___

"Physicists think in terms of pictures."
—ALBERT EINSTEIN

**PERSONAL – FINANCIAL – PROFESSIONAL
PHYSICAL – SPIRITUAL**

"True detachment isn't a separation from life but the absolute freedom within your mind to explore living."

—Ron W. Rathbun

step eight

DETACHMENT

RON W. RATHBUN

"True detachment isn't a separation from life but the absolute freedom within your mind to explore living."

"Absence of attachment to outcomes is the path to truly understanding detachment." —DARYLLE VIRGINIA DENNIS

The subject of detachment is foreign in a business setting for purposes of growing one's business and accomplishing goals. It seems incongruent to work toward increasing our business and growing our companies, while considering the concept of detachment. It is understandable why misinterpretations are prevalent in understanding what detachment means in this context.

Approaching detachment from firsthand experiences will be easier to understand and digest when placing ourselves in familiar territory. Whenever we are attached to externals for our happiness, confidence and identity, and then that external fluctuates, as it always will, then our happiness, confidence and identity fluctuate in direct proportion to the external factor.

For example, let's explore a hypothetical situation. Someone is married to a movie star, a sports star or a famous businessperson. The spouse may have decided to attach their identity and confidence to the elitism of their special circumstances and all the privileges that go with it. Suddenly, they divorce.

The divorce is the separation from their spouse and the separation from their happiness, confidence and fundamental identity, which are all going into freefall. This freefall is due to their identity attachment to the spouse and connecting the marriage to their value as a person. Maintaining one's self-identity can be challenging in this scenario. Other types of attachments also exist in our daily lives.

When we establish our value as a person attached to our careers, positions in society, status or externals of any kind, know that all externals fluctuate. That will leave our confidence and fundamental identity at risk of fluctuation as well.

Imagine the times throughout our lives when we felt confident due to an external person or situation entering our lives, and how it felt when the external was disconnected. In societies that are predominantly material, it can be nearly impossible to tune out all of the pressures to *"Keep up with the Joneses,"* should our sense of self be connected to keeping up with whomever or whatever. Each moment of the day, stresses await to pressure us to stay relevant as individuals.

The examples of the attachments to external scenarios, although only a few, represent the countless scenarios that result in the same outcomes. Externals fluctuate every time, and our identity connection to the external will fluctuate as well.

In business settings, attachments to outcomes are more commonplace on a daily basis. Companies buying companies, individuals presenting programs to companies or services to individuals, often hold an attachment to what could be considered *"a vested interest"* in the outcome. They may have a quota to fulfill, they may have financial challenges, or they may be attached to the win. Either way, there is a clear attachment to an outcome.

What is happening at a deeper level when someone is attached to an outcome?

As an example: An account executive sets an appointment with a new, potential client. Before the first meeting occurs, the account executive has determined the potential client will buy on first sight. The executive makes this decision without the permission, participation or agreement of the potential client.

The potential client will buy the program, the insurance, the mortgage, the house, the time-share: whatever is being proposed, with or without their choice. The degree of the determination of the account executive is the same degree as their attachment to the outcome.

Should the potential client not buy on first sight, the attachment to outcome sets in motion a degree of disappointment or annoyance with the person in the meeting. The account executive goes on to the next meeting with a tone of disappointment, which was self-inflicted. Detachment from outcomes sends a powerful, prosperous attitude of not needing the transactions but rather loving what we do!

Defining goals and objectives is fundamental to the success process. Going full out to be the best we can be is also fundamental to the success process. Presenting a program, a service and an opportunity with an intent to be of highest value to the situation or person is also fundamental to the success process.

How is it possible to have defined goals and results that are required or needed, and detach from the outcome? Why would detachment matter? What is the motivation to detach?

"People want to do business with people who understand them, not need them."

The personification of Value Exchange Dynamics™ addresses the dynamics present when effectiveness and productivity are at maximum efficiency.

Step Five, Access to Intuitive Intelligence, reveals our receptiveness for intuitive impulses, which provide information when making decisions and receiving solutions. Intuitive Intelligence is also where creativity and genius live.

The attachment to outcomes lowers our frequency and diminishes access to the field of intelligence and knowing. When our presence is sending out a signal of needing the transaction, the recipient feels our need at some level. Non-verbal communication happens when our focus is centered more on our receiving than on our service. This focus can potentially blind us to what is in the best interest of the client. This non-verbal communication is felt and received by the client, consciously or subconsciously; either way, it is a communication received by others.

When doing business with others, we build trust based on a sense of being heard, understood and appreciated. Once the issues and objectives are understood, introduce the product while holding in mind the best interest of the other. The quality of this interaction creates a powerful impact on both parties. An intention to be of value to another effortlessly organizes thoughts, feelings and actions automatically as a byproduct of intending value. The Intuitive Intelligence field then opens effortlessly, once again.

An intention to be of value initiates the best interest of another; no effort is needed. This prosperity practice is clearly felt and appreciated by the recipient. From that place, the potential client effortlessly chooses to move forward, giving their permission and agreement, and feeling a sense of being invited to participate in the decision.

Detachment to outcomes allows the other to make decisions for themselves. When needing the transaction and setting aside personal gain to continue to hold the best interest of the client, this is prosperity in action. Regardless of our personal situation, continuing to hold the intention for the best interest of the other will be the most astonishing path both parties are walking; both parties are benefitting. When we practice this prosperity attitude, the results will flow in effortlessly on quantum levels.

There is another aspect to detachment when considering this subject. In the goal receiving education offered in this program, Step One, Clarity, on the desired goals and objectives is essential to initiate movement and momentum.

Familiar stories are told on the subject of setting goals and receiving them, only to have a well-known phrase singing in their heads later: *"Be careful what you ask for."* Other stories are about opening up opportunities that appear to have all the earmarks of everything we ever wanted. Despite what this opportunity seems to offer, there is an intuitive sense that something is wrong. Often, we move forward anyway, denying our intuitive self, only to later regret moving forward.

Additional stories come to mind regarding desiring something so much, and for whatever reason, that something eludes us. Perhaps we hear years later that what we wanted so badly was contrary to what we thought it would be for our lives. Then we are very relieved it never happened.

Our intuition is connected to a vast field of intelligence. This intelligence has a *"knowing"* that manages from a higher, broader view of holding our best interest at all times. Intuition is a tool made available inherently within our fundamental design as human beings. When we begin listening to our *"inner voice, our inner knowing,"* we will avoid considerable time, expense, effort, struggle and disappointment by listening and responding to what our intuitive self hears and feels.

This is where detachment to outcomes begins making sense. Here is a suggested affirmation to release attachments to any outcome:

"If this opportunity happens and moves forward, it is for my best interest. If this opportunity does not happen and does not move forward, it is for my best interest."

We have countless experiences where we decide and force decisions from our own needs, and the situations do not turn out well in the big picture. Our intuitive selves have direct access to the big picture. Relying on our intuitive selves, which happens automatically when we intend value to others, will also activate a deep appreciation for ourselves. Once our identity is rooted in valuing ourselves and others, we minimize the risk of interpreting our value on any external source or person to whom we are connected.

Finally, what may serve us well is to affirm and eventually trust on the front end that no matter what the outcome, the circumstances will always prove to be for our best interest. It may be a matter of time for evidence to appear confirming *"detachment from outcome"* has worked out for the best for ourselves, our families and clients; however, the wait is well worth it, no matter what it looks like at the time.

A new normal would be requesting the highest and most benevolent outcomes for all situations and circumstances with others. This request alone unquestionably holds the connectivity to the bigger picture, while always holding our best interest at heart.

"Don't try to steer the river." —DEEPAK CHOPRA

Shortly after getting married and moving to Denver, Colorado, I learned of a former client who was now also living in Colorado and was the president of a title insurance company. Reaching out to him by phone to meet up, he said right away, *"Come and work for me!"* All I said, being somewhat surprised, was, *"Okay."*

I met with the president the next day to catch up on how we both landed in Colorado, and he said, *"Start Monday!"* I said, *"Okay."* Laughing to myself, I thought, *"He must think I am very thrifty with words!"*

Monday morning, after handling personnel matters, I went into the field to begin exploring what this territory was all about and possibly make a few cold calls. I observed a commercial business park near the office and stopped to look at their directory and see who was in the building. Seeing the name of a mortgage company, usually a wonderful client for title insurance, I decided to walk in cold and explore what was possible.

When I walked in, there was no furniture, phones were on top of phone books, and two men were sitting on the floor. I simply asked, *"Are you coming in, or are you going out?"* They laughed and shared they were opening their company that day. As strange as this sounds, they had two loans written, which required title insurance and escrow services.

First call, two deals, loving Colorado!

I did share with them, *"Yes, I work with the title company, but actually, I am a consultant and work with companies to build their sales results quickly and in quantum leaps through a practice called Value Exchange Dynamics™. If you're interested, I would be happy to support the building of your company, training your team and participating in your growth. The title business will generate significant income for my company and myself."* They were thrilled!

This was not a new idea. As a commercial business development banker, my business plan was the same. My business plan always viewed every corporate client as if they had just hired me and were paying me to be of value to them.

One of the values I could bring to their companies was growth and development, which have been passions of mine since the beginning of my career. I was not just their banker; I was a business development and marketing arm of their organization. In the totality of my career, I never lost one client to a competitor bank.

Practical Application

The business-building journey with my new client in Colorado began. After interviewing the two owners and sorting out their view of ideal clients, I began making connections for them within the real estate community. During a meeting with a realtor who was not interested in real estate any longer, I had a great idea. How perfect would it be for a former realtor who understands what other realtors are going through, now to consider approaching realtors as a mortgage agent? It turned out to be an amazing connection for the mortgage company and for this wonderful young woman!

On Saturdays, I held trainings in sales strategies and strengthening communication, as well as attitudes and belief systems. In what seemed like the blink of an eye, they were processing 180 to 200 loans a month. The title insurance company president was quite pleased when he saw premiums on an average of $65,000 to $75,000 a month from one client, regularly pouring in.

As a new salesperson for the title company, my commissions fluctuated between $8,000 and $11,250. I became the No. 1 producer on the sales team in four and a half months.

The next eight months were incredible for this new mortgage company; business was flowing, their clients were happy, their team was ecstatic and life was good!

Then one morning, as usual, I stopped by and checked on how things were going at the mortgage company. The president said to me, *"I am so glad you stopped by. I wanted to let you know that I will be splitting the business we have here between you and a girl from another title company."* I asked, *"Do you mind if I ask why you are doing this?"* To my disbelief, he said, *"Have you ever seen this girl's legs?"*

Truly thinking this was a joke, I responded, *"Surely, you are not possibly making a business decision because of someone's legs? Are there cameras behind me? Am I being punked?"*

He then replied, *"No. Not a joke. We will begin splitting the business between both of you today."* I excused myself and left.

I went to my car and sat for a while to process what was happening. Several things went through my mind: the money coming in like clockwork each month was wonderful, especially being new to Colorado; I could lose my No. 1 status; look at all I did to build the company for these two men; how shall I move forward?

All of these thoughts were attachments to outcomes. When I calmed down a bit, I had only one thought: *"I do not work with people like this."* The amount of energy that would be required to hide how I felt about this situation would not be worth any amount of money. I made the decision there and then in the car. I realized I would need to detach and let go of the concerns about losses and find another client worthy of the value I bring to every client. The decision alone was so powerful! There was a sense of such freedom. It was exhilarating to let go and detach from an identity that was connected to stuff and status.

Then, I drove directly to the office to meet with the president. Sharing the situation with him, and much to his amazement, I requested,

"I would appreciate it if you would trust me on how I would like to handle this situation. I would like to disconnect from this client and invite him to use the other title company exclusively. This is your company, and their premiums are certainly attractive. You could turn the account over to someone else, or if you trust me, allow me to say goodbye and give me just one month, and I will find another client and replace the premiums quickly." The president agreed.

At 4:30 p.m. that same day, I went into this client's office and said, *"I have reevaluated our relationship and have come to realize it is no longer a match. From this day forward, we will no longer receive any new business from your mortgage company. We will, however, complete the transactions already in motion. We will simply not take in any new transactions. Thank you for the time we spent together, and good luck to you."*

The president of the mortgage company went a bit ballistic. He called the president of the title company and demanded he take their business. The president politely said, *"No, thank you."* He then called the head of the escrow department and demanded she take their business. She politely said, *"No, thank you."* Finally, he called the head of the title department, demanding they take his business. The head of the title department politely said, *"No, thank you."*

The president of the title company and I shared a moment of humor when I later said, *"Had I known twenty-five years ago that saying, 'Hello, I am Darylle Virginia Dennis and I do not want your business' was more effective than saying 'I do want your business,' I would have changed my approach a long time ago."*

Here is the end of the story, and it shows detachment working in an amazing way. I found freedom and lightness of being, and a renewed confidence and hope for the future. Having nothing to fear was an incredible feeling. I had so much energy from detaching from the situation that I couldn't go home now. I thought I would make another cold call.

Having just left the mortgage company and saying our goodbyes, it was close to 5 p.m. I chose to go to another building in the same commercial business park to save time. Quickly, I looked at the directory in the building, only to find another mortgage company on the second floor. Leaping up the stairs, I walked in and asked for the president, who came out immediately and took time to meet, even though it was almost 5 p.m.

It turns out, that day, this president had a catastrophic experience with their title insurance company, and he had had enough and was going to begin looking for another title company the next day.

I happily saved him the time of looking and quickly set up for his company to have a special team inside our company to take care of the volume of business about to come in!

This new client would regularly produce $100,000 in premiums on a monthly basis. That is $1.2 million annually. It was a tremendous joy to be able to keep my promise to the president of my own title company and to have significantly more premiums than what we had just let go of. I made the commitment within thirty-five minutes of detaching from the previous client.

This was a profound learning experience for me. I became aware of my own attachment to outcomes and experienced how unhealthy and fragile that was, and decided to see myself in a wholly different identity. Who I am is one who contributes value in every client experience. They may stay and they may go; however, who I am is not about status or No. 1 or comfort. Who I am is about value and being of value to others, with or without money and status. The alternative, attachment, is only temporary anyway.

The money, the comfort, being the best and becoming No. 1 all feel great! I strive to be the best I can be and always to bring forth more of my potential. However, as this story suggests, when we are attached to things and define those things as *"who I am,"* that's when it's only a matter of time before our suffering begins. After all, attachment to materialism is not who we are anyway.

We're magnificent human beings, here on a journey in business dynamics, meeting people and having experiences that will build our character and our talents and gifts, while contributing value to others. The best of all journeys is the awakening of human potential! Enjoy the journey! It truly is worth it, priceless, really, due to the challenges and the lessons.

The new mortgage company client and I had a wonderful, longstanding relationship for six and a half years. Every month, I would take the president out and say, "*Thank you for the quality of my life your loyalty provides.*"

Step Eight: Detachment

"Absence of attachment to outcomes is the path to truly understanding detachment." —Darylle Virginia Dennis

_____
_____
_____
_____
_____
_____
_____
_____
_____
_____
_____
_____
_____
_____
_____
_____
_____
_____

"People want to do business with people who understand them, not need them."
—Darylle Virginia Dennis

**Personal – Financial – Professional
Physical – Spiritual**

"Gratitude is the highest state we exemplify. Dr. Emoto repeatedly revealed in studies that gratitude is the most positive influential state we have available. When we are in a state of gratitude, everything works out for the best interest of all organically. Goodness surrounds those in a grateful state. Gratitude heals judgments. A state of gratitude opens access to creativity. Gratitude is an access point for entering an Intuitive Intelligence state."

—DARYLLE VIRGINIA DENNIS

step nine

CONTRIBUTION

MAYA ANGELOU

"When you learn, teach. When you get, give."

"Gratitude is the highest state we exemplify. Dr. Emoto repeatedly revealed in studies that gratitude is the most positive influential state we have available. When we are in a state of gratitude, everything works out for our best interest organically. Goodness surrounds those in a grateful state. Gratitude heals judgments held from a long-ago past or from current disappointments. A state of gratitude opens access to creativity and solutions for circumstances impacting our lower states. Gratitude is an access point for entering an Intuitive Intelligence state." —DARYLLE VIRGINIA DENNIS

Contributing to a situation or a person who could benefit from our help is an actionable communication of gratitude not only in their life, but ultimately in the quality of our lives.

We have all experienced lending a hand when we find a situation or person in need. Habitat for Humanity is a perfect example where people come together in a group and contribute themselves in whatever ways are needed to build a house and provide a home for a family in need.

Think back to a situation, circumstance or person, and recall when your heart felt full: a child being born, the magnificence of nature, a kindness offered, a genuine loving touch or a time when your contribution made a significant difference in someone's life. Those feelings are centered in our hearts.

As shown earlier, according to Heartmath Institute, how we feel is five thousand times stronger than anything we may be thinking. Imagine the power we can generate in our hearts when we simultaneously tap into how we feel about a person or situation, and then activate a feeling of gratitude toward the person or situation. Most people who experience higher states have such overwhelming emotions and energy beyond others around them. Often, they have a sense of not being able to contain all that energy in their bodies alone.

All states that we experience, high or low, are transient and fleeting. Imagine being able to hold higher states for longer periods of time. Imagine what an extraordinary life we would have to create, to enjoy and to influence daily by being able to stay in higher states for longer. Grace and good fortune would fill up our lives.

The question may be, *"How does someone stay in higher states for longer periods? How would it be possible to be in higher states at all when living in such a fast-paced world with many pressures and stresses?"*

Yes, it is possible to stay in higher states longer through a state of gratitude. The state of gratitude does not have judgments that something is wrong and needs changing and fixing. Pressure and stress come from judgments, which come from the mind evaluating good and bad, right and wrong. A judging mind offers solutions to correct the wrongs and fix the bads.

We have all lived through at least one circumstance or situation that, at the time, seemed really bad and really wrong. *"Hindsight is 20/20 vision,"* meaning hindsight is perfect vision. This expression tells us, *"When looking back on it, if the situation hadn't happened, we wouldn't be enjoying the life we have today. Therefore, nothing was bad or wrong, only as it should be as a preparation for our future. There is always a higher harmony going on at all times. Hindsight proves this to be true."* Gratitude liberates us from judgments, and this liberation is one way to be in higher states for longer periods of time.

Evaluating through our hearts instead of through our minds means we see events happening for a reason, and that reason is for our best interest. Gratitude makes this possible. *"What makes gratitude possible?"* Contribution makes gratitude possible because contribution stimulates gratitude.

There are unlimited ways to contribute to someone or a situation. Contributions can be small kindnesses and courtesies: holding a door for someone or waving at someone to enter the lane ahead of us while driving.

Small courtesies and kindnesses keep us in a higher state as long as we have no expectations of getting something back for our kindnesses.

When we offer contributions of our presence and our time, it immediately stimulates a high state of heart and mind. We are bodies filled with energy, and the energy within us flows to others and flows from those around us. The quality of our attitude and our state of mind invigorates the energy exchanges accordingly. Intentions affect the quality of our contributions and the quality of the energy exchanges. Intentions are singularly initiating the quality of energy when expressing gratitude. The quality of our contribution begins with our intentions and attitudes. Are we contributing because of external pressures of some form? *What will it look like if I do not contribute?* Contributions are private and are choices we make ourselves.

When our contributions toward another or a situation are fully from our own reasons and our own hearts, without expectation of what we may get back, we feel a fullness of gratitude, an energy beyond words, flowing through us and from us toward others.

In essence, the privileges and qualities of our lives continue to grow and flourish without disruption when our gratitude and actions contribute to others generously as a matter of choice.

The story of the experience in Arizona with the title insurance company and the real estate community's struggles is an example of how to apply contribution as a business methodology. The title insurance company's clients were primarily realtors and mortgage loan officers who were being impacted by the decline of the real estate market. The approach was one of contribution to raise the spirits and the confidence of the discouraged group, without any expectation of what they would receive.

Contribution is a form of gratitude. The title insurance company had enjoyed ten years of business and loyal customers, and with the market decline, now had an opportunity to say thank you with their actions. Never before had this company gone into the marketplace only to contribute to the well-being of the people in the real estate and mortgage communities.

When their team members offered much-needed goodness for so many, it resulted in this title insurance company having a ten-year record-breaking result day after day after day.

Contribution

Kindnesses and generosities without expectation of returns seem to attract grace and love from unexpected sources.

PRACTICAL APPLICATION

In 2014, Ann Curry interviewed Oprah Winfrey on the Broadway stage featuring the musical *The Color Purple*. Ann Curry took the viewers behind the scenes, and toward the end of the brief tour, she sat with Oprah and questioned her about her relationship with God by asking, *"Do you pray?"* Oprah answered, *"Yes."* Ann asked, *"Do you pray once a week, every day?"* Oprah answered, *"I live in the space where God is…"*

Curry takes us on a brief taped journey, showing the magnitude of Oprah's contributions in many areas of need in the world. She describes contribution as: *"I allow myself to be guided by that which is greater than myself, than my personality. I am doing the work my soul came here to do."*

https://youtu.be/ApjsL-JrkYQ Oprah's Interview on Broadway with Ann Curry

When we contribute and give from a life position of making a difference, that is where our full potential and identity truly blossom. The best of ourselves becomes alive, and we see who we truly were born to be, and that is a magnificent view of our value and preciousness.

Intention to be of value to others as a way to be alive in each moment is *"living in the space where God is and where prayer lives."*

Oprah spoke at an event and ended with this encouragement:

> *"It's my prayer that we leave this place with the purest of intention … and the intention should be that we allow our excellence to come forth and serve the world. That's success. That's power."* —Oprah Winfrey

STEP NINE: CONTRIBUTION

"When you learn, teach. When you get, give."
— MAYA ANGELOU

_____
_____
_____
_____
_____
_____
_____
_____
_____
_____
_____
_____
_____
_____
_____
_____
_____
_____

"Don't try to steer the river."
—DEEPAK CHOPRA

**PERSONAL – FINANCIAL – PROFESSIONAL
PHYSICAL – SPIRITUAL**

Made in the USA
Middletown, DE
23 January 2025